NEVEN'S
Food from the Sun

To Amelda, who shares my passion
for food – a wonderful travelling
companion, colleague, friend
and wife. Thank you for your love
and support. Where to next?

HarperCollins Publishers Ltd.
77–85 Fulham Palace Road
London W6 8JB

www.harpercollins.co.uk

First published in 2008 by Collins

Collins® is a registered trademark of
HarperCollins Publishers Limited

Text © Neven Maguire, 2008
Photographs © David Munns, 2008

12   11   10   09   08
7   6   5   4   3   2   1

Mixed Sources
Product group from well-managed
forests and other controlled sources
www.fsc.org Cert no. SW-COC-1806
© 1996 Forest Stewardship Council

FSC is a non-profit international organisation established to promote the
responsible management of the world's forests. Products carrying the FSC
label are independently certified to assure consumers that they come
from forests that are managed to meet the social, economic and
ecological needs of present and future generations.

Find out more about HarperCollins and the environment at
www.harpercollins.co.uk/green

A catalogue record for this book is available from
the British Library

ISBN 978-0-00-728513-6

Editorial Director: Jenny Heller
Project Editor: Ione Walder
Copy Editor: Gillian Haslam
Photography: David Munns
Design: Nicky Barneby
Cover: Anna Martin

Colour reproduction by Colourscan
Printed and bound in Italy by Lego

Contents

Introduction 7

SMALL BITES: APPETISERS, MEZZE AND TAPAS 8

POULTRY 34

MEAT 58

FISH 82

VEGETABLES AND SALADS 108

DAIRY AND EGGS 136

PULSES, GRAINS AND PASTA 156

SWEET THINGS 184

LARDER 210

Acknowledgements 220

Index 221

Introduction

I love travelling. Every January my wife, Amelda, and I head away to far flung places. In recent years we have been to Laos, Thailand, Vietnam, Australia, Bali and the USA. And wherever we go I love to sample the local food – tasty Thai noodles, rich Moroccan tagines, spicy Mexican food, delicious Italian pasta, fresh Greek salads and so much more. There are many wonderful new tastes, flavours and ingredients out there to discover.

I also enjoy visiting the local markets, such as the amazing Sineu village in Palma, Mallorca. There is a lot of pleasure to be had in finding exotic vegetables, rifling through enormous sacks of spices and sampling local cheeses and meats. And I love to get down to the ports to see the boats coming in and the freshest fish on offer. In this book I wanted to draw on some of these holiday moments with recipes based on dishes I enjoyed abroad – for you to cook at home.

The food we eat is constantly changing and developing. People are becoming more adventurous. Supermarkets are stocking ever increasing ranges of exotic ingredients and excellent fresh food, and great specialist stores are popping up everywhere. You should have no difficulty finding all the ingredients in my recipes. Those holiday flavours no longer have to be just a distant memory.

No matter how much cooking experience you have, the food you serve is only as good as the ingredients you use and I like to buy local, seasonal produce and to support my local suppliers who provide fresh, top quality goods. Your butcher and fishmonger will offer better value than anything pre-packed and they are experts when it comes to preparing meat and fish exactly how you want it. They are worth a visit.

Each of the nine chapters in the book is themed around a different type of ingredient. There are ideas for whatever is in your fridge whether you're preparing breakfast, a quick supper, a barbecue or a special occasion family feast. I have also included a larder chapter; a good basic stock is essential as the body and soul of so many soups and sauces.

Holiday dining is always pleasurable – you get to enjoy the sun while someone else cooks your lunch! I enjoy the change for a while but honestly I am never happier than when I am cooking. To help you to revive those memories I have tried to keep the recipes in this book as straightforward as possible. A few require that extra bit of effort, but I think they are definitely worth it. Join me in these new tastes, flavours and combinations, all with the memory of holidays and that hint of the sun.

Happy Cooking!

Neven

small bites:
appetisers, mezze and tapas

Oven-roasted Dublin Bay Prawns (Langoustines)
with Tomato and Chilli

Serves 4

900g (2lb) ripe tomatoes, peeled (see page 119), halved and seeded

1 small red chilli, halved and seeded

1 small onion, peeled and roughly chopped

1 red pepper, halved, seeded and roughly chopped

1 large garlic clove, peeled

small handful of fresh flat-leaf parsley and basil leaves

2 tbsp olive oil

100g (4oz) Serrano ham slices, finely shredded

25g (1oz) plain flour

large pinch of sweet paprika

12 raw large Dublin Bay prawns (langoustines), shelled and left whole

Maldon sea salt and freshly ground black pepper

chopped fresh flat-leaf parsley, to garnish

1 lemon, cut into wedges

crusty bread, to serve

This dish is a great example of Spanish cuisine – the unique flavours of the ingredients enhance but do not smother each other. I was inspired to make this by Gillian Bowler, when she was a contestant on RTE's *The Restaurant*. King prawns would also work well instead of Dublin Bay prawns.

Preheat the oven to 180°C (350°F), gas mark 4. Place the tomatoes, chilli, onion, red pepper, garlic clove and herbs in a food processor. Pulse until finely chopped.

Heat 1 tablespoon of the olive oil in a frying pan set over a medium heat, add the tomato mixture and season with salt and pepper to taste. Gently fry for 30 minutes, stirring occasionally, until reduced and thickened. Transfer to an ovenproof dish, then stir in the Serrano ham.

Mix the flour and paprika in a shallow bowl and lightly coat the prawns in the mixture. Heat the remaining oil in a very hot frying pan and quickly sear the prawns on both sides until golden brown. Place them in the ovenproof dish on top of the sauce and drizzle over any oil left in the frying pan. Roast for 6–8 minutes or until the prawns are just cooked through and slightly firm. Garnish with parsley and serve at once with lemon wedges and a separate basket of crusty bread to mop up all the delicious juices.

Roasted Red Pepper and Chilli Hummus
with Crispy Tortilla Chips

Serves 4–6 | VEGETARIAN

1 large red pepper

olive oil, for cooking

1 red chilli (mild)

400g can of chickpeas, drained and rinsed

juice of 1 lemon

2 garlic cloves, peeled and crushed

good pinch of ground cumin

100ml (3½fl oz) tahini (sesame seed paste), optional

2 tbsp extra-virgin olive oil

pinch of sweet or smoked paprika

Maldon sea salt and freshly ground black pepper

roughly chopped fresh flat-leaf parsley, to garnish

For the tortilla chips

4–6 soft flour tortillas

olive oil, for brushing

This variation on traditional hummus has a fantastic, vibrant colour. Here it is served with home-cooked crispy tortilla chips, which are much lower in fat than the ones you buy. It's also great spread on crackers or chunks of warm bread, or scooped up with toasted garlic bread.

Preheat the oven to 200°C (400°F), gas mark 6. To prepare the tortilla chips, place two baking trays in the oven for about 5 minutes until well heated. Meanwhile, brush both sides of the soft flour tortillas with olive oil, then cut in half. Cut each half into four triangles and arrange on the heated baking sheets. Place in the oven for 3–4 minutes until crisped up.

Place the whole red pepper in a roasting tin and drizzle with a little olive oil. Roast in the oven for 15 minutes, then add the whole chilli and drizzle over a little more olive oil. Continue to cook for another 15–20 minutes until both vegetables are completely tender and nicely charred. Transfer to a plastic food bag and leave to cool completely. This will help to steam the skins off. When cool enough to handle, peel both, cut in half and remove the cores and seeds. Roughly chop the flesh.

Place the red pepper and chilli flesh in a food processor with the chickpeas, lemon juice, garlic, cumin, tahini (if using) and 4 tablespoons of water. Blend to a creamy purée. Taste, then add more lemon juice, garlic, cumin or some salt if needed. Turn out into a wide serving bowl, and smooth the surface with the back of a spoon. Drizzle with the extra-virgin olive oil and sprinkle over a little paprika and freshly ground black pepper. Garnish with the parsley. To serve, arrange the crispy tortilla chips on a platter next to the bowl of roasted red pepper and chilli hummus.

VARIATION

Avocado Hummus

Instead of the red pepper and chilli, you will need one ripe
avocado. Hass avocados are available all year round and have
a lovely creamy texture, but other varieties are also fine to use.
Cut the avocado in half, remove the stone and scoop out the
flesh into the food processor with the rest of the ingredients.
Proceed with the final stage of the recipe as described opposite.

Halloumi with Griddled Pitta
and Red Onion, Bean and Tomato Salad

Serves 4 | VEGETARIAN

I first enjoyed halloumi while on holiday in Cyprus, where it has been produced for centuries. It is a semi-hard cheese prepared from the milk of sheep, cows or goats and then sometimes rolled in wild mint. It has a distinct and pleasant flavour and is versatile to cook with, as its soft springy texture always retains its shape even when fried or grilled.

To prepare the salad, place the garlic, lemon rind and juice and olive oil in a large pan set over a low heat, stirring to combine. Stir in the haricot beans with the tomatoes, red onion, olives and herbs, add salt and pepper to taste, then leave to warm gently for 5 minutes. Remove from the heat and place in a bowl to marinate for 1 hour, which will allow the flavours to develop.

When ready to cook the halloumi, heat a griddle pan and a frying pan, until both are very hot. Cut the halloumi cheese into four thick slices and dip them in cold water, then dust all over with the paprika. Add the olive oil to the heated frying pan, then add the halloumi slices. Fry for 4 minutes, turning once, until golden. Remove the pan from the heat and squeeze the lemon juice over the cheese.

Meanwhile, arrange the pitta bread on the griddle pan or under a preheated grill and cook for 1 minute, turning once until puffed up and lightly charred. Alternatively, put the pitta in a toaster for a minute or two. Cut into slices on the diagonal.

Spoon the red onion, bean and tomato salad into the centre of four plates and arrange a piece of grilled halloumi on top, spooning over the lemon-flavoured pan juices. Arrange the griddled pitta slices on the side to serve.

250g (9oz) halloumi cheese

1 tsp sweet or smoked paprika

1 tbsp olive oil

juice of ½ lemon

4 white pitta bread

For the salad

1 garlic clove, peeled and crushed

finely grated rind and juice of ½ lemon

1 tbsp extra-virgin olive oil

400g can of haricot beans, drained and rinsed

12 vine cherry tomatoes, halved

1 small red onion, peeled and diced

12 pitted black olives

1 tsp chopped fresh flat-leaf parsley

1 tsp chopped fresh mint

Maldon sea salt and freshly ground black pepper

Bruschetta Platter

Serves 4–6

Warm grilled breads with various toppings appear all over the Mediterranean, and make the perfect nibble at a drinks party. The key to success with this dish is to use the finest-quality ingredients. Splash out on the best extra-virgin olive oil and get some lovely rustic bread, or if you're really lucky you might be able to find wood-fired sourdough.

12 thick slices of rustic bread, preferably sourdough

1 garlic clove, peeled and halved

4 tbsp extra-virgin olive oil

To prepare your bruschetta, preheat the grill to medium or heat a griddle pan and use to toast the slices of bread on both sides. Remove the toast from the heat and immediately rub one side with a piece of garlic.

Drizzle over the olive oil and cut any very large slices of toast in half. Use immediately with a selection of the delicious toppings that follow. Arrange on large serving platters or trays to serve.

Goat's cheese with fig and onion marmalade

VEGETARIAN

Heat the olive oil in a large pan and sauté the sliced red onions until softened. Stir in the chopped figs, crushed garlic, red wine and the balsamic vinegar. Simmer for about 10 minutes until most of the liquid has evaporated, then stir in the teaspoon of caster sugar and the thyme. Season to taste and leave to cool completely, then spread onto the prepared bruschetta. Thinly slice the goat's cheese and arrange on top. Place briefly under the grill until the cheese is lightly melting and brown on top. ◐

2 tbsp olive oil

3 red onions, peeled and thinly sliced

225g (8oz) ready-to-eat dried figs, finely chopped

2 garlic cloves, peeled and crushed

1 small glass red wine

2 tbsp balsamic vinegar

1 tsp caster sugar

good pinch of chopped fresh thyme

salt and freshly ground black pepper

450g (1lb) goat's cheese with rind

300g jar of artichoke hearts
in olive oil (or 400g can of
artichoke hearts in water)

handful of flat-leaf parsley

50g (2 oz) freshly grated
Parmesan cheese

juice of ½ lemon

2 tbsp extra-virgin olive oil

salt and freshly ground black
pepper

Artichoke and Parmesan purée

Drain the artichoke hearts and place in a food processor with the
flat-leaf parsley, Parmesan cheese and the lemon juice. Blitz to
form a smooth paste, then with the motor still running, slowly add
the olive oil until well combined. Add salt and pepper to taste,
then spread thickly over the prepared bruschetta.

12 slices Parma ham

12 asparagus spears,
blanched (plunged into
boiling water for 1 minute,
then rinsed)

For the tapenade

250g (9oz) pitted black olives

juice of 1 lemon

2 tbsp chopped capers

6 anchovy fillets, chopped

1 garlic clove, peeled and
crushed

2 tbsp chopped fresh flat-leaf
parsley

2 tbsp extra-virgin olive oil

salt and freshly ground black
pepper

Parma ham-wrapped asparagus with tapenade

To make a rough-textured tapenade, chop the black olives and
mix in a bowl with the lemon juice, capers, anchovy fillets,
crushed garlic and the chopped parsley. Season with salt and
pepper and add enough olive oil to form a fairly thick paste.
Spread each slice of Parma ham with some of the tapenade and
then wrap the slices around the blanched asparagus spears.
Spread the rest of the tapenade over the prepared bruschetta and
put the Parma ham-wrapped asparagus spears on top.

Roasted Aubergine and Cumin Soup

Serves 4–6 | VEGETARIAN

The silky texture of aubergine makes this a particularly rich and creamy soup. At only 150 calories per serving, it's also the perfect low-fat option.

3 large aubergines

4 tbsp extra-virgin olive oil

2 red peppers

1 large onion, peeled and finely chopped

4 garlic cloves, peeled and finely chopped

½ tsp cumin seeds

900ml (1½ pints) vegetable stock (see page 213)

salt and freshly ground black pepper

Preheat the oven to 200°C (400°F), gas mark 6. Cut the aubergines in half lengthways and trim off the stalks. Brush the cut sides with a little of the oil and sprinkle lightly with salt and pepper. Place cut-side up in a roasting tin along with the whole red peppers and bake for 30–35 minutes or until the flesh of the aubergine is tender and the skin of the red pepper is blackened and blistered.

Remove the vegetables from the oven, put the peppers in a plastic food bag and leave to cool completely. Meanwhile, roughly chop the cooked aubergines, place in a food processor and blend to a purée. Transfer to a bowl and set aside. Once the peppers are cool, remove from the bag, peel away the skin and chop the flesh, discarding the seeds. Place in a food processor and whiz until smooth.

Heat a tablespoon of the remaining olive oil in a large saucepan set over a medium heat. Sauté the onion and garlic for 2–3 minutes until they are softened but not browned. Stir in the cumin seeds and cook for another minute, stirring constantly. Add the roasted aubergine purée and the stock, stirring to combine. Cook over a low heat for 15 minutes until the flavours are well combined and the mixture is heated through. Season with salt and pepper to taste.

Purée the soup with a hand-held blender and ladle into deep soup bowls. Spoon the red pepper purée into the centre and swirl it gently into the soup. To serve, drizzle lightly with the remaining olive oil.

Crispy Fried Squid
with Harissa and Crème Fraîche

Serves 4

about 1.2 litres (2 pints) vegetable oil, for deep-frying

450g (1lb) medium-sized squid, cleaned

2 tbsp cornflour

3 tbsp fine semolina

2 tbsp sesame seeds

1 tsp ground paprika

2 tsp harissa paste

120ml (4fl oz) crème fraîche

1 medium-hot red chilli (optional), thinly sliced on the diagonal

2 spring onions (optional), trimmed and thinly sliced on the diagonal

salt and freshly ground black pepper

In Spain there is a type of flour milled especially for frying, called *harina de trigo*. The closest equivalent in the UK and Ireland is finely ground semolina. For this recipe it's crucial not to overcook the squid or it will become tough and rubbery.

Pour the oil into a large, heavy-based saucepan or wok and set over a high heat. Alternatively, heat a deep-fat fryer to 190°C (375°F). Cut the body pouch of each squid open along one side and score the inner side with the tip of a small, sharp knife into a fine criss-cross pattern, being careful not to cut all the way through the flesh. Then cut each pouch in half lengthways, then across into 5cm (2in) pieces. Separate the tentacles into pairs.

Put the cornflour, semolina, sesame seeds, paprika and a teaspoon of salt into a plastic food bag. Add the prepared squid, close the bag and shake and toss to coat. Tip out onto a tray, knocking off any excess coating, and leave for 1–2 minutes so that the cornflour mixture becomes slightly damp. This will give a crispier finish.

When the oil is hot enough (it should sizzle fiercely when you drop in a small cube of white bread), fry the squid in batches for 1–2 minutes until it is covered in a crunchy golden coating. Drain on kitchen paper.

Meanwhile, mix together the harissa and crème fraîche in a small bowl and add salt and pepper to taste. Tip the squid onto a serving plate and sprinkle over some chilli and spring onions if you wish. Place the harissa and crème fraîche dip alongside to serve.

Chicken and Wild Mushroom Wontons
with Chinese Black Bean Sauce

Serves 6

This is one of the most popular starters in my restaurant. Packets of wonton wrappers can be found in specialist Asian stores, good delis and even some large supermarkets. The wontons are cooked in two stages, first poached and then steamed; if you don't have a steamer, you could just place them in a pan of boiling water.

To make the sauce, place the black beans in a bowl and cover with hot water, then leave to soak for 5 minutes. Meanwhile, place the balsamic vinegar in a large saucepan with the sugar, tomato ketchup and soy sauce. Cook on a high heat for 1 minute, stirring, then reduce the heat to low, stir in the beef stock and simmer for 10–15 minutes until reduced and thickened. Drain and add the beans, return to a simmer and season with salt and pepper. Remove from the heat, leave to cool completely, then cover with clingfilm and set aside until needed.

To prepare the mushrooms for the filling, heat the olive oil in a large frying pan. Add the garlic, shallots and mushrooms, stir to combine, then add the butter and sauté for 5 minutes. Stir in the Madeira or port, 1 tablespoon of the cream and half the herbs. Season with salt and pepper and leave to cool.

Place the chicken breast in a food processor with two of the eggs, half of the mushroom mixture and the remaining cream. Add two pinches of salt and blend to make a smooth mousse. Place the mousse in a bowl, then stir in the rest of the mushrooms and herbs. Mix well to combine and season to taste.

Bring a large pan of salted water to the boil and keep it boiling while you assemble the wontons. Lay out 18 wonton wrappers on a clean work surface. Beat the remaining egg in a small bowl with a little water to make an egg wash. Brush the edges of each wrapper with the egg wash, then place a teaspoon of the chicken mixture into the centre of each one, being careful not to overfill. Bring all the edges up to meet in the middle and pinch together firmly to seal. ◗

2 tbsp olive oil

1 garlic clove, peeled and crushed

2 shallots, peeled and diced

175g (6oz) mixed mushrooms (such as shiitake, chestnut and chanterelle), finely chopped

1 tbsp butter, softened

1 tbsp Madeira or ruby port

120ml (4fl oz) double cream

2 tbsp chopped fresh mixed herbs (such as chives, basil and flat-flat parsley)

1 large skinless chicken breast fillet, diced

3 eggs

1 packet wonton wrappers (contains about 30 square wrappers), thawed if frozen

1 pak choi

1 tbsp toasted sesame oil

salt and freshly ground black pepper

For the black bean sauce

2 tbsp Chinese black beans

1 tbsp balsamic vinegar

1 tbsp light muscovado sugar

1 tsp tomato ketchup

1 tbsp dark soy sauce

300ml (10fl oz) beef stock (see page 212)

The wontons are now ready to poach. Put them into the boiling water as soon as possible after filling them and poach for about 2 minutes until cooked through and floating at the top.

The next stage is to steam the wontons, although this can be done up to 24 hours later. If you are preparing the wontons in advance, lay them out in a single layer on a tray and leave to cool. Cover with clingfilm and chill. Otherwise, you can steam them immediately.

When ready to steam, arrange the wontons in a single layer in a steamer and cook for about 5 minutes until heated through. If you don't have a steamer, put the wontons in a large pan of boiling water, cover with a lid and allow to cook for 4–5 minutes.

Separate the leaves of the pak choi and trim down the stalks. Slice each leaf in half lengthways, then plunge into boiling water for 30 seconds; drain well. Heat the sesame oil in a large frying pan or wok and toss the pak choi until just tender and nicely glazed. Season with salt and pepper.

Arrange some of the pak choi on each warmed plate, along with three of the steamed wontons. Add a small dish of the black bean sauce on the side of each plate to serve.

Vietnamese Spring Rolls
with Plum Sauce

Serves 4–6

The perfect starter for any Oriental-themed meal! (See the photograph on page 22.) In Vietnam, the rolls generally contain minced pork, but here I've used prawns for a different result. They're easy to make and the specialist spring-roll wrappers and preserved plums can be bought from Chinese grocers and some larger supermarkets. You can use two ripe fresh plums, with the stones removed, if you prefer.

To make the plum sauce, place 225ml (8fl oz) of water in a heavy-based saucepan with the sugar, vinegar, plums and some salt. Bring to the boil, then lower the heat and simmer until the liquid has reduced by about a quarter. Remove from the heat and stir in the chopped coriander, then use a hand-held blender to mix to a smooth sauce. Transfer to a serving bowl and allow to cool.

Place the noodles in a large bowl and cover with boiling water. Leave for about 5 minutes until softened or according to the packet instructions. Rinse in cold water and, using kitchen scissors, snip the noodles into small lengths. Set aside.

Place the fresh coriander in a mini blender or pestle and mortar with the garlic and white pepper. Blend or pound to a paste, then transfer to a bowl. Stir in the prawns with the fish and soy sauces, then set aside for 5 minutes to allow the flavours to combine.

Cut the wrappers into quarters to make twenty-four 6cm (2½in) squares. Place a tablespoon of the prawn mixture near one corner of each square, fold in both sides on the diagonal and roll up tightly. Brush a small amount of the beaten egg yolk onto the open end and press the edge closed to seal the spring roll. Repeat with the rest of the wrappers and the remaining prawn mixture.

Place the rolls on a rack until ready to fry. Add the oil to a wok or deep-sided pan and heat until very hot and slightly smoking. Gently drop in as many rolls as will fit in one layer. Carefully fry them for 2–3 minutes until golden brown. Drain on kitchen paper.

Place a hot spring roll on each lettuce leaf and garnish with mint. To eat, wrap the rolls in the lettuce and dip into the plum sauce.

25g (1oz) vermicelli rice noodles

7g (¼oz) bunch of fresh coriander, including the roots

1 garlic clove, peeled and crushed

1 tsp freshly ground white pepper

250g (9oz) raw tiger or Dublin Bay prawns (langoustines), peeled, de-veined and chopped

1 tsp Thai fish sauce

1 tsp light soy sauce

6 x 25cm (10in) spring-roll wrappers, thawed if frozen

2 egg yolks, beaten

about 1.2 litres (2 pints) groundnut oil, for deep-frying

24 iceberg or Webb lettuce leaves, trimmed, and fresh mint leaves, to serve

For the plum sauce

100g (4oz) caster sugar

2 tbsp rice wine vinegar

6 Chinese preserved plums, rinsed if in brine

pinch of salt

1 tbsp roughly chopped fresh coriander

Aubergine and Mozzarella Parcels
with Pesto and Sun-dried Tomatoes

1 large aubergine

120ml (4fl oz) extra-virgin olive oil

2 garlic cloves, peeled and crushed

finely grated rind of 1 lemon

1 ripe beef tomato

2 x 100g (4oz) balls of mozzarella cheese

about 2 tbsp basil pesto

8 sun-dried tomatoes in olive oil, drained and halved

salt and freshly ground black pepper

lightly dressed rocket salad (see page 100), to serve

8 cocktail sticks

These are great for a barbecue, as a starter or an exciting side dish with any kind of meat. They can be made in advance and simply popped on the barbecue just before you want to eat. You could also replace the mozzarella with feta or halloumi.

Trim off the stalk end of the aubergine, then cut lengthways into eight slices, 5mm (¼in) thick, discarding the ends. Arrange the slices in a single layer on a large baking sheet.

Preheat a griddle pan until very hot, or prepare a barbecue with medium–hot coals. Mix together the olive oil, garlic and lemon rind in a small bowl, season with salt and pepper, then brush the mixture over the aubergine slices. Place the aubergine on the heated griddle pan or the barbecue and cook for 2–3 minutes on each side until charred. Be careful not to cook for any longer or the aubergine will become too soft. Remove from the heat and leave to cool a little.

Slice the top and bottom off the tomato and cut the rest into four thick slices, then cut each slice in half again to make eight pieces in total. Cut each mozzarella ball into four slices. Place the cooked aubergine slices on a clean work surface and place a piece of tomato in the middle of each slice. Arrange a slice of mozzarella on top, then add a small dollop of the basil pesto. Arrange the sun-dried tomatoes on top and season with salt and pepper. Flip over both ends of the aubergine to enclose the filling and secure each parcel with a cocktail stick.

Brush the outside of each parcel with the rest of the garlic and lemon oil and return to the griddle pan or barbecue for 1–2 minutes on each side or until they are heated through and lightly golden. Again, be careful not to overcook. To serve, arrange on warmed plates with the rocket salad.

Cracked Patatas Bravas

Serves 4 | VEGETARIAN

This is a Spanish tapas favourite and every tapas bar tends to have its own version. It makes a delicious snack in its own right, but is also a fantastic accompaniment to Butterflied Poussin (see the photograph on page 49) or with Blackened Chicken with Roasted Red Pepper and Avocado Salsa (page 41).

Wrap the baby new potatoes in a clean tea towel and hit them gently with a wooden mallet or rolling pin to crack them lightly. Flatten each garlic clove in the same way.

Heat the olive oil in a large frying pan and cook the onion for a minute or two to soften. Tip in the cracked potatoes and garlic and continue to cook for 10–12 minutes until golden, stirring regularly.

Sprinkle the chilli flakes over the potato mixture along with the paprika and sugar. Season with salt and pepper and give everything a good stir to coat the potatoes evenly. Fold in the tomatoes and tomato purée and bring to a gentle simmer.

Cover the frying pan with a lid (a large enough plate would also do the job) and simmer for 15 minutes, stirring every 5 minutes or so to ensure that the mixture cooks evenly, until the potatoes are completely tender and coated in a thick tomato sauce. Stir in the basil and then tip into warmed individual bowls, or serve as a side dish.

675g (1½lb) baby new potatoes, scrubbed

4 garlic cloves, unpeeled

2 tbsp olive oil

1 red onion, peeled, halved and thinly sliced

good pinch of dried chilli flakes

½ tsp sweet or smoked paprika

good pinch of dark muscovado sugar

400g can of chopped tomatoes

1 tbsp sun-dried tomato purée

1 tbsp torn fresh basil leaves

Maldon sea salt and freshly ground black pepper

Chicken Satay
with Pickled Cucumber Salad

Serves 4

4 tbsp dark soy sauce

2 tsp clear honey

2 tsp medium curry powder

450g (1lb) skinless chicken fillets, cut into long strips

salt and freshly ground black pepper

For the pickled cucumber salad

4 tbsp rice wine vinegar

2 tbsp caster sugar

large pinch of salt

½ small cucumber, peeled, halved, seeded and thinly sliced

For the dipping sauce

2 tbsp crunchy peanut butter

2 tsp dark soy sauce

1 tsp light muscovado sugar

juice of ½ lime

120ml (4fl oz) coconut milk

½ red chilli, seeded and finely diced

2 tbsp chopped fresh coriander

6 wooden skewers (15cm (6in) in length), soaked

This is a classic South-East Asian street food that I enjoyed on a recent trip to the region. Satay has a wonderful balance of sweet and spicy flavours that penetrate the chicken. It is perfect for cooking on the barbecue; just make sure you soak the skewers first.

First prepare the pickled cucumber salad. Place the vinegar in a bowl and stir in the sugar and salt until dissolved. Tip in the sliced cucumber, stir to combine and set aside to allow the flavours to develop.

Preheat a griddle pan until smoking hot, or preheat the grill. Whisk together the soy sauce, honey and curry powder in a bowl. Season with salt and pepper and stir in the chicken pieces. Leave to marinate for a few minutes.

Meanwhile, make the dipping sauce. Heat the peanut butter in a small saucepan over a low heat and stir in the soy sauce, sugar and lime juice. Gradually whisk in the coconut milk until you have achieved a smooth sauce. Stir in the chilli and coriander, then leave to cool.

Thread the chicken pieces onto the pre-soaked wooden skewers and arrange on the griddle pan or under the grill. Cook for 4–6 minutes, turning once or twice, until cooked through.

Arrange the chicken satay skewers on warmed plates. Divide the dipping sauce between individual ramekins and place to one side of the skewers. Drain the pickled cucumber salad, add to the plates and serve at once.

Poached Oysters
with Spinach and Lemongrass

Serves 4

16 oysters (Pacific if available)

25g (1oz) butter

225g (8oz) fresh spinach leaves, washed and tough stalks removed

For the lemongrass sauce

1 tsp softened butter

1 shallot, peeled and finely chopped

2 lemongrass stalks, outer leaves removed and core finely chopped

finely grated rind and juice of 1 lemon

150ml (5fl oz) dry white wine

100ml (3½fl oz) double cream

salt and freshly ground white pepper

This is the perfect recipe if you want to try cooking or eating oysters for the first time. It might sound fancy, but it's actually very easy and guaranteed to impress your guests. You can ask your fishmonger to remove all the oysters from their shells or follow the instructions below.

Scrub the oyster shells thoroughly. Place an oyster on a tea towel on a firm surface, flattest shell uppermost and hinge towards you. Gather the tea towel around the oyster and grip it firmly so there is a thick wad of cloth protecting your hand. With the other hand, insert an oyster knife or a sharp rigid blade into the gap in the hinge and twist upwards to snap the shells apart. Slide the blade along the inside of the upper shell to sever the muscle that keeps the shells together. Lift off the top shell and run the knife under the oyster to remove it from the bottom shell. Repeat with the rest of the oysters. Clean the bottom shells and reserve for serving.

To make the lemongrass sauce, melt the butter in a saucepan set over a medium heat. Add the shallot, lemongrass and lemon rind and cook for 2–3 minutes until softened but not browned, stirring occasionally. Pour in the wine and simmer until reduced by half, stirring at intervals. Stir in the cream and bring to the boil, then turn down the heat and simmer for 5 minutes until slightly reduced and thickened. Season with salt and pepper and stir in the lemon juice. Blitz with a hand-held blender and pass through a fine sieve into a clean saucepan. Keep warm over a low heat.

Just before you poach the oysters, melt the butter in a large pan and add the spinach and a pinch of salt. Cook for a minute or so over a high heat until just wilted, then drain off any excess liquid and spoon a mound of spinach into each oyster shell. Arrange on heated plates and keep warm. Add the oysters to the warm lemongrass sauce, still over a low heat, and gently poach for 30 seconds, but no longer. Carefully remove the oysters with a slotted spoon and place on top of the spinach in the shells. Place the hand-held blender in the sauce and blitz to lighten, then spoon the sauce over the poached oysters to serve.

Marinated Olives

Serves 4 | VEGETARIAN

In my opinion, the best type of olives for this dish come from Italy and have been stored in olive oil. You'll find them at farmers' markets or in a good deli. The longer you leave them to marinate, the better the flavour will be.

Toast the cumin and fennel seeds in a small, dry frying pan for 1–2 minutes until they become aromatic. Tip into a bowl and add the olives, lemon rind and juice, garlic, chillies, if using, and olive oil.

Toss until each olive is well coated and either drain off the excess liquid immediately and tip into small bowls to serve, or leave to marinate and allow the flavours to develop for as long as possible. The olives can be prepared up to one week in advance and stored in a bowl covered with clingfilm in the fridge.

1 tsp cumin seeds

1 tsp fennel seeds

225g (8oz) black or green olives, or a mixture

finely grated rind and juice of 1 small lemon

2 garlic cloves, peeled and crushed

1 tsp dried crushed chillies (optional)

4 tbsp extra-virgin olive oil

Spiced Glazed Almonds

Serves 4 | VEGETARIAN

These crunchy spiced nuts make an excellent snack to go with a few drinks. I like to use almonds but cashew nuts or pecan halves also work well.

Heat the oil in a frying pan set over a medium heat and add the almonds, stirring to coat. Sprinkle over the sugar, paprika and pepper. Cook for about 5 minutes, stirring constantly, until the almonds are golden brown and the sugar has caramelised.

Spread out on a baking sheet to cool and harden, then break up any clusters as necessary before piling into small bowls to serve.

1 tbsp olive oil

225g (8oz) roasted salted whole almonds

4 tbsp caster sugar

1 tsp sweet or smoked paprika

1 tsp freshly ground black pepper

poultry

Turkey Moussaka

175ml (6fl oz) olive oil, for cooking

1 large onion, peeled and finely chopped

3 garlic cloves, peeled and finely chopped

750g (1¾lb) lean minced turkey

175ml (6fl oz) white wine

¼ tsp ground cinnamon

¼ tsp ground allspice

1 tbsp chopped fresh oregano

2 bay leaves

1 tsp fresh thyme leaves

2 x 400g cans of chopped tomatoes

4 medium aubergines

plain flour, for dusting

salt and freshly ground black pepper

Chunky Greek Salad, to serve (see page 111)

For the cheese sauce

75g (3oz) unsalted butter

75g (3oz) plain flour

900ml (1½ pints) milk

75g (3oz) Parmesan cheese, freshly grated

100g (4oz) Gruyère cheese, grated

1 egg, plus 2 egg yolks

Moussaka is a Greek dish made up of layers of minced lamb and aubergine, covered with a cheese sauce. Here, I've used turkey instead, which is economical and quite low in fat, but you could always make it the traditional way if you prefer. There are a few stages to the recipe, so it is best prepared in advance and then cooked just before serving.

Heat 2 tablespoons of olive oil in a large flameproof casserole dish. Add the onion and cook gently for 6–8 minutes, stirring at intervals. Stir in the garlic and cook for another 2–3 minutes, stirring occasionally, until the onion is softened but not browned.

Put a little olive oil in a frying pan set over a fairly high heat, then tip in half the minced turkey. Cook until lightly browned, breaking up any lumps with a wooden spoon, then empty onto a plate. Repeat until all of the turkey is cooked, then deglaze the pan by adding just a little white wine and scraping the base of the pan with a wooden spoon to loosen any sediment, allowing the liquid to simmer until it has reduced slightly.

Stir the cinnamon, allspice, oregano, bay leaves and thyme into the casserole dish with the onion mixture and cook for about a minute, stirring. Add the cooked turkey and the reduced wine, along with the remaining wine and the chopped tomatoes. Bring to the boil, then lower the heat and simmer for 45–50 minutes until the turkey has broken right down and the liquid has reduced.

Meanwhile, cut the aubergines into slices 1cm (½in) in thickness and layer them up in a colander, sprinkling with salt between each layer. Set aside on the draining board for 30 minutes to allow the salt to draw out any bitter juices.

To make the cheese sauce, melt the butter in a large non-stick saucepan set over a low heat and stir in the flour. Remove the pan from the heat and gradually whisk in the milk, then return to the heat and cook for 6–8 minutes, stirring continuously, until the sauce is smooth and thick. Remove from the heat again and stir in 50g (2oz) of Parmesan and 50g (2oz) of Gruyère until melted. ◗

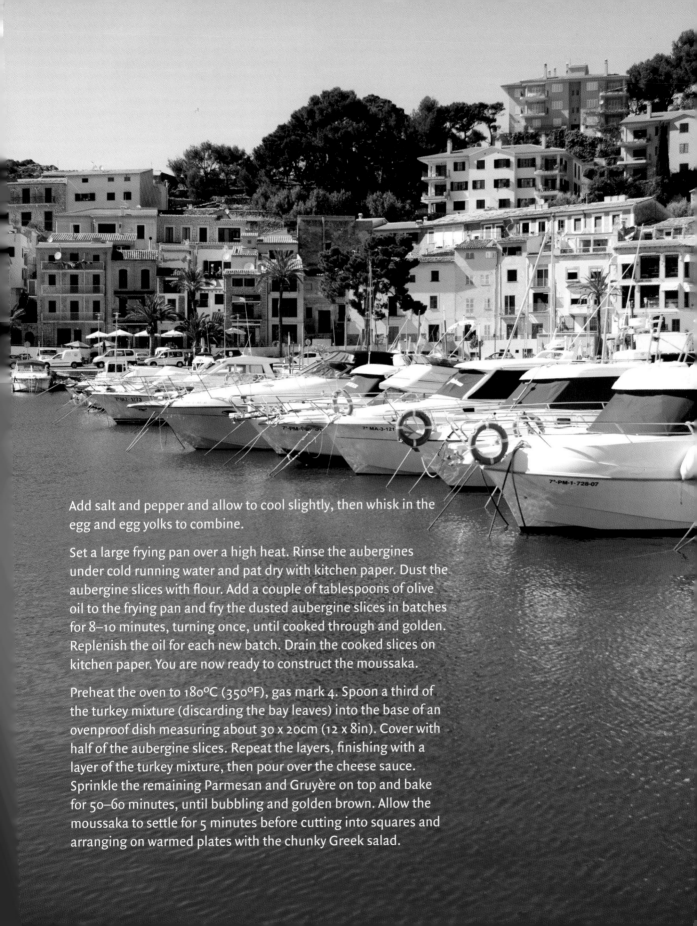

Add salt and pepper and allow to cool slightly, then whisk in the egg and egg yolks to combine.

Set a large frying pan over a high heat. Rinse the aubergines under cold running water and pat dry with kitchen paper. Dust the aubergine slices with flour. Add a couple of tablespoons of olive oil to the frying pan and fry the dusted aubergine slices in batches for 8–10 minutes, turning once, until cooked through and golden. Replenish the oil for each new batch. Drain the cooked slices on kitchen paper. You are now ready to construct the moussaka.

Preheat the oven to 180°C (350°F), gas mark 4. Spoon a third of the turkey mixture (discarding the bay leaves) into the base of an ovenproof dish measuring about 30 x 20cm (12 x 8in). Cover with half of the aubergine slices. Repeat the layers, finishing with a layer of the turkey mixture, then pour over the cheese sauce. Sprinkle the remaining Parmesan and Gruyère on top and bake for 50–60 minutes, until bubbling and golden brown. Allow the moussaka to settle for 5 minutes before cutting into squares and arranging on warmed plates with the chunky Greek salad.

Spicy Chicken and Mango Noodles

450g (1lb) skinless chicken fillets

100g (4oz) vermicelli rice noodles

1 red onion, peeled and thinly sliced

small bunch of fresh coriander

handful of fresh mint leaves

1 ripe mango, peeled, stone discarded and cut into fine strips

4 tbsp roughly chopped toasted cashew nuts

For the marinade

1 tbsp dark soy sauce

1 tbsp sweet chilli sauce

juice of ½ lime

1 tsp mild curry powder

1 garlic clove, peeled and crushed

pinch caster sugar

2 tbsp torn fresh basil leaves

2 tbsp sunflower oil

For the dressing

1 tsp caster sugar

2 tbsp dark soy sauce

1 tbsp sweet chilli sauce

juice of 1 lime

4 tbsp sunflower oil

This quick light salad is perfect for eating alfresco, whether you decide to cook the chicken under the grill or on a barbecue. Tiger prawns would make a nice alternative to the chicken.

Place all the ingredients for the marinade in a non-metallic bowl and mix well to combine. Cut the chicken fillets into 3cm (1¼in) strips and stir into the marinade. Cover with clingfilm and chill for at least 2 hours or overnight to allow the flavours to penetrate the chicken.

To make the dressing, dissolve the sugar in the soy sauce in a small bowl, then whisk in the sweet chilli sauce, lime juice and sunflower oil.

Place the vermicelli noodles in a large bowl and cover with boiling water. Leave for about 5 minutes until softened or according to the packet instructions.

Put the red onion slices in a bowl of iced water for 2–3 minutes – this will make them crisp and will tone down the flavour a little.

Drain both the vermicelli and red onion well and place together in a large bowl. Tear the coriander and mint leaves away from their stalks and add to the bowl along with the mango strips and cashew nuts.

Preheat the grill to high. Shake any excess marinade from the chicken strips and place the meat on a foil-lined grill rack. Cook for 5 minutes, turning once or twice.

To serve, add the cooked chicken and the dressing to the bowl with the noodles and toss until well combined.

Blackened Chicken
with Roasted Red Pepper and Avocado Salsa

Serves 4

This dish is a favourite of mine during barbecue season. If you make a double quantity of the spice mixture and keep it in an airtight container in the fridge for a week or two, you'll be ready to marinate any meat that you are grilling. The salsa also tastes great with grilled or barbecued fish.

Mix together the chilli powder, paprika, garlic salt (if using), thyme and parsley with half the olive oil in a shallow non-metallic dish. Add 2 teaspoons of black pepper and half a teaspoon of salt to season. Add the chicken breasts and rub the mixture into the flesh. Leave for a couple of hours or, if time allows, cover with clingfilm and chill overnight to let the flavours penetrate the flesh.

To roast the pepper for the salsa, preheat the oven to 220°C (425°F), gas mark 7 and roast the pepper in a small tin for 20–25 minutes until the skin is black. Alternatively, spear the stalk end of the pepper on a fork and hold over the flame of a gas hob, turning regularly until the skin has blistered and blackened, or scorch the pepper with a chef's blowtorch. Leave to cool and then break in half and remove the stalk, skin and seeds; discard. Cut the flesh into small dice and place in a bowl.

Preheat the grill to high. Arrange the chicken fillets on the grill rack and cook for about 8 minutes on each side, basting with the remaining oil until the chicken is lightly charred and just tender (you could also cook these on a barbecue or griddle pan).

To finish the salsa, put the chilli oil, garlic and red chilli into a small frying pan and, as soon as it starts to sizzle, pour it onto the roasted red pepper mixture, stirring to combine thoroughly. Add the lime juice and herbs and season with salt and pepper. Cut the avocado in half and peel off the skin, then dice the flesh, discarding the stone. Fold into the salsa and set aside.

Transfer the rested blackened chicken to a chopping board and slice on the diagonal. Arrange on plates with the roasted red pepper and avocado salsa. Garnish with the parsley sprigs to serve.

1 tsp chilli powder

1 tsp sweet paprika

1 tsp garlic salt (optional)

1 tbsp chopped fresh thyme

1 tbsp chopped fresh flat-leaf parsley, plus extra sprigs to garnish

4 tbsp olive oil

4 x 200g (7oz) large skinned chicken breast fillets, at room temperature

salt and freshly ground black pepper

For the salsa

1 large red pepper

1 tbsp chilli oil (see page 219 or shop-bought)

1 garlic clove, peeled and crushed

1 medium-hot red chilli, seeded and finely chopped

juice of 1 lime

1 tbsp chopped fresh mixed herbs (such as coriander and parsley)

1 ripe avocado

Chicken and Broad Bean Paella
with Clams

Serves 6–8

1.2 litres (2 pints) chicken stock (see page 215)

½ tsp saffron strands, soaked in a little warm water

about 120ml (4fl oz) olive oil

175g (6oz) raw chorizo, peeled and thinly sliced

100g (4oz) pancetta, diced

8 skinless, boneless chicken thighs, well trimmed and each cut in half

2 garlic cloves, peeled and finely chopped

1 large Spanish onion, peeled and finely diced

1 red pepper, seeded and diced

1 tsp fresh thyme leaves

½ tsp dried chilli flakes

425g (15oz) Spanish short-grain rice (such as *Calasparra*)

1 tsp sweet paprika

120ml (4fl oz) dry white wine

350g (12oz) fresh broad beans, podded and shelled

4 ripe vine tomatoes, peeled, seeded and diced

18 large clams (such as *palourde*), cleaned

2 tbsp chopped fresh flat-leaf parsley

salt and freshly ground black pepper

This is one-pot dining at its best, and looks very special cooked in a *paellera* (the traditional paella dish). I brought one home from Spain a number of years ago and, despite lots of use, it is still in perfect condition.

Put the stock and saffron in a large saucepan set over a high heat and bring to the boil. Then turn the heat down to keep the stock warm but not boiling. Heat half the olive oil in a paella dish or large, heavy-based sauté or frying pan. Add the chorizo and pancetta and fry for a few minutes until crisp and lightly golden, then transfer to a plate and set aside. Put the chicken pieces in the pan and fry for a few minutes on each side until golden; remove and set aside with the chorizo and pancetta.

Add half the remaining olive oil to the pan. Add the garlic, onion and pepper and cook for a few more minutes, stirring at intervals.

When the vegetables have softened but not browned, add the thyme, chilli flakes and rice to the pan and stir for about 2 minutes or until all the grains of rice are nicely coated and glossy. Stir in the paprika, then pour in the wine and allow it to bubble a little. Pour in the hot, saffron-infused chicken stock, then stir in the cooked chorizo, pancetta and chicken thighs and cook for about 5 minutes, stirring occasionally.

Fold in the broad beans and tomatoes and season with salt and pepper. Place the clams on top of the paella so that they will open facing upwards and continue to cook gently for another 10–15 minutes or until the rice is just tender. Discard any clams that have not opened. Remove from the hob and leave the paella to rest in a warm place for 10 minutes. Garnish with the parsley and serve straight from the paella dish.

Tea-smoked Barbary Duck

Serves 4

Barbary duck is far less fatty than traditional English duck. For a really special occasion you could even experiment with game, such as guinea fowl or pheasant, for this recipe.

50g (2oz) loose jasmine tea leaves

50g (2oz) light muscovado sugar

50g (2oz) long-grain rice

4 x 225g (8oz) Barbary duck breasts, well trimmed, skin left on

4 tsp sesame oil

1 tbsp hoisin sauce

1 tsp sweet chilli sauce

1 tsp dark soy sauce

jasmine rice and Stir-fried Baby Pak Choi with Mushrooms (see page 128), to serve

spring onion, shreds of red chilli, to garnish the rice

Scrunch the sides of a foil circle to make a container about 12.5cm (5in) in diameter. Mix the tea, sugar and rice, pour into the foil dish and place in the base of a wok with a tight-fitting lid. Using a sharp knife, lightly criss-cross the skin of each duck breast. Brush each one all over with a teaspoon of sesame oil and arrange on a rack that will fit in the wok. Don't yet put the rack into the wok.

Place the wok (containing the tea) over a very high heat. When the tea starts smoking, add the rack of duck breasts. Cover with the lid and leave on the heat for 10 minutes. Don't be tempted to look under the lid as the smoke will disperse and the duck won't cook. If lots of smoke is escaping into your kitchen, or your smoke alarm goes off, turn the heat down a little.

After 10 minutes, remove the wok from the heat but still don't lift the lid. Let it cool for 5 minutes and the smoke to dissipate slowly, then transfer the duck to a plate and allow to cool completely. It is now smoked and just needs a final cooking.

Preheat the oven to 200°C (400°F), gas mark 6. Heat a large ovenproof frying pan over a moderate heat. When the pan is hot, add the duck breasts, skin-side down, and cook for 1–2 minutes until the skin is crisp and golden brown.

Meanwhile, mix together the hoisin, sweet chilli and soy sauce in a small bowl. Remove the pan from the heat and drain off the excess fat. Brush the fillet side of each breast with a teaspoon of the hoisin mixture, then turn the fillets over so that they are skin-side up. Transfer the pan to the oven and cook for another 5–6 minutes if you like your duck pink, a bit longer for well done.

Leave the duck to rest for a couple of minutes, then carve each breast on the diagonal and fan out on hot plates. Serve with a mound of pak choi and a bowl of jasmine rice. Scatter the rice with the spring onions and chilli shreds.

Creamy Chicken Korma

Serves 4

This authentic recipe from my good friend Naseem Booth is one that I return to again and again. Curries always taste better when they have been kept for a day or two. This one will keep quite happily in the fridge for two days, and also freezes very well.

Heat the oil in a large saucepan and fry the onions and garlic until for about 10 minutes until golden brown. Stir in the ginger and green chilli and cook for 1 minute, stirring.

Add the garam masala to the pan with the turmeric, chilli powder and a pinch of salt and cook for another minute, stirring. Add the tomatoes, tomato purée and 150ml (5fl oz) of water, stir well to combine, then reduce the heat and simmer for 20–25 minutes, stirring occasionally, until the sauce is so well reduced that it is almost sticking to the bottom of the pan and the oil has separated out on the surface.

Add the chicken to the sauce with a few tablespoons of water. Slowly bring to the boil, then reduce the heat and simmer gently with the lid on for about 20 minutes or until the chicken is cooked through and completely tender. Stir in the cream and simmer gently for a few more minutes until well combined. Season with salt and pepper.

To serve, spoon basmati rice and chicken korma onto warmed plates and scatter over the coriander. Place the naan breads in a separate serving dish to pass around with the mango chutney.

2 tbsp sunflower oil

2 onions, peeled and finely chopped

2 garlic cloves, peeled and crushed

2 tsp finely grated root ginger

1 green chilli, seeded and finely chopped

1 tsp garam masala

1 tsp ground turmeric

¼ tsp chilli powder

400g can of chopped tomatoes

1 tsp tomato purée

4 boneless skinless chicken breasts, cut into 2.5cm (1in) cubes

150ml (5fl oz) double cream

salt and freshly ground black pepper

2 tbsp roughly chopped fresh coriander, to garnish

basmati rice, warmed naan bread and mango chutney, to serve

Butterflied Poussin

Serves 4–6

1 tbsp mixed peppercorns

4 poussins, butterflied (ask your butcher or see method for instructions)

4 large garlic cloves, peeled and finely chopped

finely grated rind of 2 large oranges

2 handfuls of fresh basil leaves

4 spring onions, trimmed and finely chopped

1 red chilli, seeded and finely chopped

2 tbsp clear honey

2 tbsp fino (dry) sherry

150ml (5fl oz) olive oil

salt and freshly ground black pepper

lightly dressed green salad, to serve

8 metal skewers (23cm (9in) in length)

Poussins are the smallest type of chicken you can buy. I like them because they are tender and quick to cook but you could use any type of chicken pieces instead. As the poussin cooks it will blacken in places, resulting in a well-flavoured, crisp skin and moist, tender meat underneath.

Place the peppercorns in a small frying pan and toast for a few minutes, tossing occasionally, until aromatic. Grind to a powder in a mini blender or with a pestle and mortar, then set aside.

If your butcher hasn't already butterflied the poussins, use poultry shears or kitchen scissors to cut each poussin down both sides of the backbone, then remove and discard the bone. Snip the wishbone in half, open out the poussin, then snip out the ribs. Turn skin-side up, and press down firmly on the breastbone with the heel of your hand to flatten out. Trim off any excess skin, wash under cold running water and pat dry with kitchen paper.

Place the garlic, ground peppercorns, orange rind, basil, spring onions and chilli in a mini blender or pestle and mortar and work into a smooth paste. Transfer to a large plastic container with a lid and add the honey, sherry and olive oil. Season with salt and pepper and stir until well combined. Add the butterflied poussins and turn to coat them thoroughly in the mixture, then secure the lid and leave to marinate in the fridge for at least 4 hours or preferably overnight, shaking the container occasionally.

When ready to cook, either preheat the grill to medium–hot or the oven to 220°C (425°F), gas mark 7. Thread two metal skewers in a criss-cross fashion through each butterflied poussin, wiping off any excess marinade. This keeps them flat during cooking – it also makes them easier to handle when hot.

Arrange the poussins on a grill pan or a large roasting tin with a wire rack, and cook for 10–15 minutes on each side until cooked through and golden brown, basting occasionally with the leftover marinade. Leave to rest for a few minutes, then remove the skewers and arrange on warmed plates with some green salad.

Vietnamese-style Grilled Five-spice Chicken Thigh Salad

Serves 4

Chicken thighs are not only cheaper than breasts but they can result in a much tastier dish. The secret of this recipe is in the slow cooking, which would leave a breast fillet tasteless and dry. When using thighs, you end up with crispy skin and succulent, well-flavoured flesh.

To make the marinade, place the garlic in a mini blender or a pestle and mortar, along with the shallot, ginger and sugar, then work to a paste. Transfer to a small bowl and whisk in the soy sauce, Thai fish sauce, five-spice powder and several grinds of black pepper.

Arrange the chicken thighs in a shallow, non-metallic dish and pour over the marinade, turning the meat until well coated. Cover and chill for at least 2 hours or up to 24 hours for best results, turning the chicken thighs several times in the marinade. Bring back to room temperature before cooking and wipe off any excess marinade with kitchen paper.

Heat a frying pan over a medium heat. Put the oil in the pan, then add the chicken thighs skin-side down. Cook for 20–30 minutes until the skin is golden and crispy. Don't be tempted to touch them while they are cooking or to shake the pan – just leave them alone and they will cook beautifully.

When the chicken thighs are browned and the flesh is almost (but not quite) cooked through, turn them over and fry for another 5–6 minutes until completely cooked through and tender. Remove from the heat and leave to rest in a warm place for 5 minutes.

Plunge the green beans into a pan of boiling salted water for 1 minute until just tender, then drain and refresh under cold running water. Place the salad leaves in a large bowl with the blanched beans, red pepper and tomatoes. Add salt and pepper to taste and lightly dress the salad with vinaigrette. Toss well and divide between plates, then carve the chicken thighs into pieces and place on top. Garnish with the carrot shreds and chives.

6 garlic cloves, peeled and sliced

1 large shallot, peeled and roughly chopped

1 tbsp minced or chopped fresh root ginger

4 tsp caster sugar

4 tbsp dark soy sauce

4 tbsp Thai fish sauce (*nam pla*) or light soy sauce

½ tsp Chinese five-spice powder

8 chicken thighs, with skin

2 tbsp sunflower oil

100g (4oz) green beans, trimmed and sliced into 2.5cm (1in) lengths

275g (10oz) mixed salad leaves

1 small red pepper, halved, seeded and diced

225g (8oz) cherry plum tomatoes, halved or quartered

2–3 tbsp vinaigrette (see page 85)

salt and freshly ground black pepper

very fine shreds of carrot and long thin fresh chives, to garnish

Thai Yellow Chicken Curry

50g (2oz) fresh coriander

4 shallots, peeled and chopped

2 garlic cloves, peeled and chopped

2 tbsp sunflower oil

2 tbsp Thai yellow curry paste

2 x 400ml cans of coconut milk

225ml (8fl oz) chicken stock (see page 215)

12 boneless, skinless chicken thighs, cut into bite-sized pieces

2 tbsp Thai fish sauce (*nam pla*) or light soy sauce

grated rind and juice of 1 lime

1 tbsp caster sugar

good handful of fresh basil leaves, roughly torn

salt and freshly ground black pepper

Thai fragrant rice and lime wedges, to serve

Thai curries are very quick and easy to prepare. If you want, you could try making your own curry paste (see page 104), although I don't usually bother because most supermarkets sell very authentic ready-made pastes. I like to serve this curry with Thai fragrant rice, which has a characteristically soft and slightly sticky texture.

Remove about a quarter of the coriander leaves from the stalks and reserve. Roughly chop the remainder, including the stalks and place in a mini blender or pestle and mortar with the shallots and garlic. Work into a paste.

Heat a wok or heavy-based frying pan. Add the oil and stir-fry the yellow curry paste for 1 minute over a high heat. Add 150ml (5fl oz) of coconut milk along with the coriander paste, stirring well to combine. Cook for 2 minutes, then add the chicken stock and boil for 8–10 minutes, stirring occasionally, until the natural oils start to separate on the surface. Season generously with salt and pepper.

Stir in the chicken, reduce the heat and simmer for 15 minutes or until the chicken is completely tender and the sauce has reduced considerably, with the oils again clearly visible on the surface.

Add the remaining coconut milk, the soy or fish sauce, lime rind and juice and the sugar, bring to a simmer and cook for another 5 minutes. Add the reserved coriander leaves and the basil and cook for another minute or two. Serve hot with bowls of rice and lime wedges.

Thai Green Prawn Curry

Replace the yellow curry paste with green. Add 175g (6oz) of halved baby new potatoes instead of the chicken and simmer for 15 minutes until tender. Add 450g (1lb) raw peeled tiger or Dublin Bay prawns (langoustines) and 100g (4oz) halved cherry tomatoes and cook for another 2–3 minutes until the prawns are just cooked through and tender. Stir in a handful of torn basil leaves before serving.

Thai Red Duck Curry

Replace the yellow curry paste with red. Instead of the chicken, add 675g (1½lb) Peking duck breasts with the skin removed and cut into bite-sized pieces. Cook as described opposite and finish with coriander leaves before serving.

Crispy Shredded Chinese Duck Salad

1 whole aromatic duck (Silver Hill or similar)

½ head iceberg lettuce, core discarded and leaves shredded

1 firm, ripe mango, peeled, stone removed and cut into thin strips

4 spring onions, trimmed and thinly sliced

50g (2oz) roasted cashew nuts, roughly chopped

good handful of fresh coriander leaves

For the dressing

120ml (4fl oz) sunflower oil

4 tbsp rice wine vinegar

2 tbsp hoisin sauce

1 tsp caster sugar

1 tbsp finely minced or chopped fresh root ginger

1 garlic clove, peeled and crushed

½ tsp toasted sesame oil

salt and freshly ground black pepper

Now that authentic Chinese aromatic duck is readily available in major supermarkets, this salad is very quick and easy to prepare. The duck can be cooked a couple of hours ahead of time, so all you have to do is toss the ingredients together just before you're ready to serve.

Preheat the oven to 200°C (400°F), gas mark 6. Remove the duck from its packaging and place on a rack over a roasting tin. Roast for 1½ hours or according to the instructions on the packet, until the skin is crisp and the duck is completely heated through. Remove from the oven and leave to rest for 20 minutes.

Carve the meat from the duck and cut into bite-sized pieces, discarding the bones and any excessively fatty pieces of skin. Place in a large bowl with the lettuce, mango, spring onions, cashew nuts and coriander.

To make the dressing, place the sunflower oil in a small bowl with the vinegar and hoisin sauce. Whisk until blended, then stir in the sugar, ginger, garlic and sesame oil. Season with salt and pepper.

Toss the salad lightly in the dressing until evenly coated. Arrange on plates and serve the remaining dressing in a small jug so that your guests can help themselves.

Turkey Enchiladas
with Chilli Sauce

2 tbsp chilli oil (see page 219 or shop-bought)

1 tbsp hot chilli powder

1 tbsp paprika

pinch of caster sugar

grated rind and juice of 1 lime

4 skinless turkey breast fillets, cut into strips

2 tbsp sunflower oil

1 red onion, peeled, halved and sliced

1 red and 1 yellow pepper, halved, seeded and thinly sliced

8 soft corn or flour tortillas

100g (4oz) Cheddar cheese, grated

handful flat-leaf parsley, roughly chopped

lightly dressed green salad, to serve

For the chilli sauce

2 tbsp sunflower oil

1 onion, peeled and finely chopped

2 garlic cloves, peeled and crushed

1 red chilli, seeded and finely chopped

½ tsp sweet or smoked paprika

½ tsp ground cumin

¼ tsp ground coriander

400g can chopped tomatoes in rich tomato juice

squeeze of lemon juice

salt and freshly ground black pepper

In my opinion, this Mexican dish is the perfect Friday evening family supper and tastes much nicer than any takeaway. I always keep a packet of flour tortillas in the cupboard – they often come in handy. The sauce will keep happily in the fridge for up to a week.

Mix together the chilli oil, chilli powder, paprika, sugar, lime rind and juice in a shallow, non-metallic dish. Add the turkey to the chilli mixture and stir until well coated, then cover with clingfilm and leave to marinate in the fridge for 1–2 hours.

To make the chilli sauce, heat the oil in a large pan and fry the onion for 6–8 minutes until golden. Stir in the garlic, chilli, paprika, cumin and coriander and cook for 1 minute, stirring. Add the tomatoes, lemon juice and some salt and pepper. Simmer gently for 10–15 minutes until slightly reduced and thickened.

To prepare the turkey filling, heat the sunflower oil in a wok or large frying pan. Sauté the onion and peppers for about 5 minutes until softened and just beginning to brown. Tip in the marinated turkey and continue to sauté for 3–4 minutes until the turkey is just tender and cooked through.

Preheat the oven to 180ºC (350ºF), gas mark 4. Put a mound of the turkey and pepper mixture in the centre of each tortilla, then roll up and lay side by side in an ovenproof dish. Spoon over the chilli sauce and scatter the cheese on top. Bake for 15–20 minutes until bubbling and golden brown. Sprinkle the parsley over and serve at once with a separate bowl of green salad.

Harissa Roast Chicken
with Roasted Sweet Potatoes

Serves 4

A great way to jazz up a traditional favourite. The chicken is marinated in yoghurt and spices and then rubbed with harissa, a fiery hot, deep red paste from North Africa. Harissa is made from chillies, red pepper, tomato, saffron, coriander, cayenne and sometimes cumin and caraway. It is sold in tubes, cans and jars from supermarkets and good delis.

Preheat the oven to 200°C (400°F), gas mark 6. To make the marinade, cut the garlic bulb in half horizontally and place both halves in a small roasting tin. Drizzle the cut sides with a little olive oil and roast for 40 minutes or until golden and the cloves inside are soft and squishy. Leave to cool, then squeeze the garlic out from the skin into a bowl. Add the cumin, coriander, saffron, harissa paste and Greek yoghurt. Mix well and season with salt and pepper.

Rub the marinade over the chicken, both inside and out. Put the chicken in a large plastic food bag, or place in a non-metallic dish and cover with clingfilm. Leave to marinate in the fridge for at least 4 hours, or up to 24 hours for best results.

Preheat the oven to 180°C (350°F), gas mark 4. Place the chicken in a roasting tin, cover loosely with foil and roast for 30 minutes.

Meanwhile, toss the cut sweet potatoes in the olive oil. Remove the foil from the chicken and add the sweet potatoes to the tin, then return to the oven uncovered for another 30 minutes or until the chicken is deep golden and cooked through and the sweet potatoes are lightly caramelised and tender. Let the chicken rest for 10 minutes before you carve it, then arrange on plates with the roasted sweet potatoes.

1.5kg (3lb 5oz) chicken

4 sweet potatoes, peeled and cut into large chunks

1 tbsp olive oil

For the marinade

1 whole garlic bulb

1 tbsp olive oil

1 tbsp ground cumin

2 tsp ground coriander

large pinch of saffron threads

4 tbsp harissa paste

250ml (9fl oz) Greek yoghurt

Maldon sea salt and freshly ground black pepper

TRADITION · ARLES
PORC, BOEUF
25,00 KG

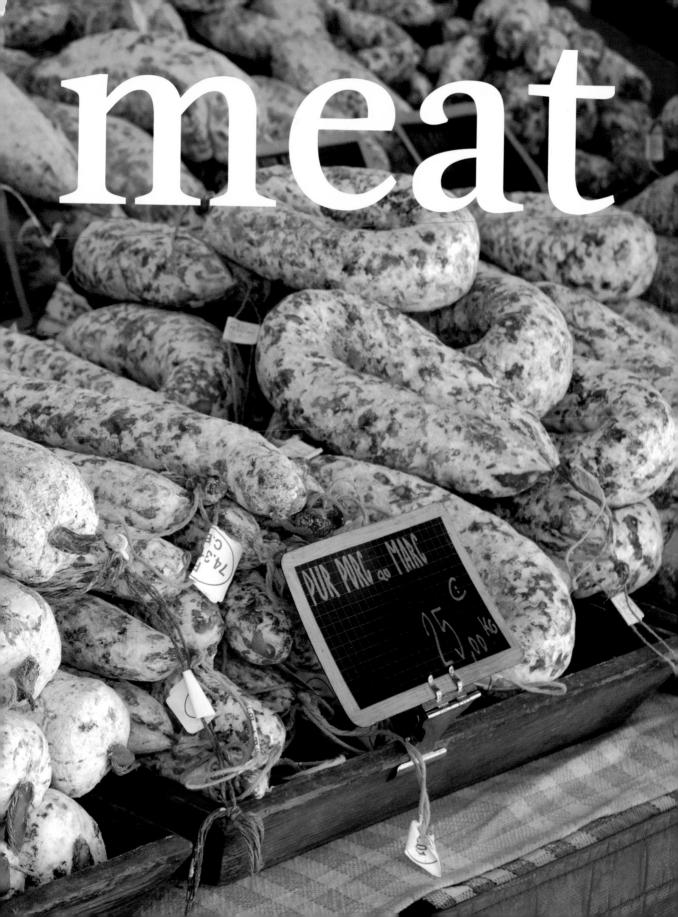

meat

PUR PORC au MARC
€
25,00 KG

Chilli Cornbread Pie

This dish is perfect for all the family. The recipe is very simple but the surprising addition of cocoa powder gives the pie a wonderful flavour and just a hint of sweetness.

Heat half the oil in a large sauté or frying pan set over a medium heat. Add the onion, garlic, celery and chilli and sauté for 5 minutes or until softened but not browned. Stir in the spices and continue to cook for 1 minute, stirring constantly.

Add the minced beef and sauté for about 5 minutes until lightly browned, breaking up any lumps with a wooden spoon. Stir in the cocoa powder, if using, along with the tomatoes, stock and kidney beans, then season with salt and pepper. Bring to the boil, then reduce the heat and simmer gently for 1 hour or until the sauce has slightly reduced.

Preheat the oven to 180°C (350°F), gas mark 4. Place the cornmeal in a bowl with the flour, baking powder and a teaspoon of salt. Stir to combine, then make a well in the centre and quickly whisk in the remaining oil, the buttermilk or yoghurt and the eggs to make a smooth, thick batter.

Spoon the chilli mince into the bottom of a deep ovenproof dish and pour over the cornmeal mixture in an even layer. Bake for 35–40 minutes in the middle of the oven until just golden brown and a skewer inserted into the centre comes out clean. Serve at once with a mixed leaf salad.

4 tbsp sunflower oil

1 large onion, peeled and finely chopped

2 garlic cloves, peeled and finely chopped

1 celery stick, diced

1 red chilli, seeded and finely chopped

1 tsp ground cumin

1 tsp ground coriander

1 tsp cayenne pepper

pinch of ground cinnamon

450g (1lb) lean minced beef

1 tbsp unsweetened cocoa powder (optional)

400g can of chopped tomatoes

450ml (15fl oz) chicken or vegetable stock (see pages 215 and 213)

2 x 400g cans of red kidney beans, drained and rinsed

150g (5oz) yellow cornmeal (or quick-cook polenta)

150g (5oz) self-raising flour, sifted

2 tsp baking powder

2 eggs, lightly beaten

300ml (10fl oz) buttermilk or Greek yoghurt

salt and freshly ground black pepper

lightly dressed mixed leaf salad, to serve

Lamb Shanks Osso Bucco

3 tbsp olive oil

50g (2oz) plain flour

4 lamb shanks

1 large onion, peeled and finely chopped

2 large garlic cloves, peeled and finely chopped

4 carrots, peeled and chopped

2 celery sticks, chopped

2 tsp chopped fresh rosemary

2 tsp chopped fresh thyme

1 bay leaf

300ml (10fl oz) dry white wine

2 tbsp tomato purée

1.5 litres (2½ pints) lamb stock (from stock cubes is fine) or chicken stock (see page 215)

1 strip lemon rind, pared with a potato peeler

salt and freshly ground black pepper

2 tbsp chopped fresh flat-leaf parsley, to garnish

mashed potato, to serve

This recipe takes its inspiration from *Ossobuco alla Milanese*, an Italian dish of braised veal shanks. I've used lamb shanks instead because they are extremely good value for money. The muscle sinews and ligaments melt away during the braising process to create a magnificent rich texture and deep flavours.

Heat 2 tablespoons of the oil in a deep, flameproof casserole dish large enough to hold all the lamb shanks comfortably. Season the flour and place in a plastic food bag, then add the lamb shanks and shake until well coated. Take out, shake off any excess flour and add to the heated casserole. Fry until nicely browned on all sides. Transfer to a plate.

Add the remaining tablespoon of oil to the casserole dish, then tip in the onion, garlic, carrots, celery, rosemary, thyme and bay leaf and fry until lightly golden. Add the wine and cook rapidly until reduced by half, scraping the bottom of the pan to loosen any sediment.

Return the lamb shanks to the casserole dish and add the tomato purée, stock and lemon rind and season to taste. Bring to the boil, then reduce the heat and simmer for 2 hours until the lamb shanks are completely tender and the sauce has slightly reduced, turning the shanks every now and then and skimming off the excess fat from the surface of the sauce occasionally. To serve, scatter the parsley over the lamb shanks and serve directly from the casserole dish with generous dollops of mashed potato.

Barbecued Brine Pork Chops
with Balsamic Glaze

Serves 4

This homemade brine is very potent – after just one day's soaking, these pork chops are seasoned all the way through. Take care not to overcook and they will be succulent beyond compare. The sugar in the brine also helps the chops to brown beautifully.

To make the brine, place the salt, sugar, garlic, thyme and pepper in a large saucepan with 2 litres (3½ pints) of water. Place over a medium heat and bring just to a simmer, stirring to dissolve the sugar and salt. Remove from the heat and transfer to a non-metallic container large enough to hold both the brine and the pork chops. Leave the brine to cool completely, then chill in the fridge until completely cold.

Add the pork chops to the cold brine, making sure they are submerged. If necessary, top the pork chops with a plate to weigh them down. Cover tightly with clingfilm and chill for 24 hours.

Remove the pork chops from the brine and pat dry with kitchen paper, then allow to come back up to room temperature. Light a barbecue or heat a griddle pan and brush it with a little olive oil. Cook the chops over medium–hot coals or on the griddle set over a medium heat for about 10 minutes until nicely browned. Turn the chops over and cook for another 10–12 minutes until cooked through and tender.

Heat a separate frying pan. Add a knob of the butter, then sauté the shallots for 2 minutes until softened but not browned, stirring occasionally. Add the vinegar, then bring to the boil and boil fast until reduced by half. Add the stock and sage and return to the boil, stirring constantly. Cook for another 5–10 minutes until reduced by just over half. Remove from the heat and swirl in the remaining butter.

4 centre-cut loin pork chops, each about 4cm (1½in) thick

olive oil, for brushing

50g (2oz) unsalted butter, diced and chilled

2 large shallots, peeled and very finely chopped

2 tbsp balsamic vinegar

225ml (8fl oz) chicken stock (see page 215)

1 tbsp chopped fresh sage

wilted spinach, to serve (see page 77)

For the brine

100g (4oz) Maldon sea salt

50g (2oz) light muscovado sugar

4 garlic cloves, peeled and halved

small bunch of fresh thyme leaves

1½ tsp coarsely ground black pepper

Caramelised Pork Belly
with Mustard Potato Purée

Serves 6

1 tbsp olive oil

2kg (4½lb) pork belly, boned, rolled and tied with string

2 carrots, peeled and diced

1 onion, peeled and diced

600ml (1 pint) red wine

1.2 litres (2 pints) beef stock (see page 212)

600ml (1 pint) apple juice

2 fresh thyme sprigs

2 fresh rosemary sprigs

2 garlic cloves, peeled and crushed

4 tbsp clear honey

4 tbsp dark soy sauce

salt and freshly ground black pepper

roasted root vegetables, to serve (optional)

For the rosemary and Madeira jus

1 tbsp balsamic vinegar

1 heaped tsp tomato purée

pinch of light muscovado sugar

1 tsp chopped fresh rosemary

2 tbsp Madeira or ruby port

For the mustard potato purée

1kg (2¼lb) floury potatoes, peeled and cut into chunks

150ml (5fl oz) double cream

50g (2oz) butter

1 tsp wholegrain mustard

2 tbsp apple sauce

1 tbsp snipped fresh chives

This is a very gutsy, full-flavoured dish with more than a hint of influence from the Far East. It's one of the most popular dishes in my restaurant. Ask your butcher for pieces of pork belly that are 5–7.5cm (2–3in) thick. Go for slabs from the front belly, and which have about a 50/50 balance of lean meat to fat. Ensure that they are well trimmed and then rolled and tied with string.

Preheat the oven to 160°C (325°F), gas mark 3. Heat the olive oil in a large, heavy-based pan set over a high heat. Add the rolled pork belly and brown all over, turning regularly. Transfer to a casserole dish and set aside. Put the diced carrots and onion in the pan and cook for 5 minutes until golden brown, stirring regularly to ensure they cook evenly.

Tip the vegetables over the seared pork belly, then stir in the red wine, beef stock, apple juice, herbs and garlic. Cover with a lid or foil and bake for 3 hours until the pork belly is cooked through and the juices run clear when a skewer is inserted into the middle. Remove from the oven and leave to sit for 1 hour in the braising juices, then remove, cut the string and wrap the pork in a double layer of kitchen foil. Leave to cool, then store in the fridge for a minimum of 8 hours or, for very best results, up to 24 hours. This makes the meat much easier to slice, otherwise it is likely to crumble apart. Strain the braising juices through a fine sieve and reserve for making the jus.

To reheat the pork belly, heat a large frying pan over a high heat. Cut the pork into six even-sized slices. Mix together the honey and soy sauce in a small bowl and pour into the pan. Add the pork slices and warm through, basting in the juices, for 4–5 minutes until caramelised.

To make the jus, place the vinegar in a heavy-based saucepan with the tomato purée, sugar, rosemary and Madeira. Reduce by half, then add the reserved braising juices and simmer for about 15 minutes until reduced and thickened, stirring occasionally. Add seasoning and keep warm or reheat as needed. ❍

Place the potatoes in a large saucepan of salted water and bring to the boil. Reduce the heat and simmer for 15–20 minutes until the potatoes are tender. Drain well, then mash until smooth. In a separate pan, heat together the cream, butter, mustard and apple sauce, then stir into the mashed potatoes to make a smooth purée. Season with salt and pepper and stir in the chives.

To serve, place a large spoonful of the potato purée in the centre of each warmed bowl and carefully arrange the caramelised pork belly on top. Drizzle over the rosemary and Madeira jus and serve with a separate dish of roasted root vegetables, if liked.

Parma-wrapped Pork Fillet
stuffed with Pesto

Serves 4

2 x 400g (14oz) pieces of pork fillet, trimmed

6 0 12 thin slices of Parma or Serrano ham, about 225g (8oz) in total   *132 5*

salt and freshly ground black pepper

Oven-baked Tomatoes (see page 129), to serve

For the pesto

100g (4oz) pine nuts

large bunch fresh basil, leaves stripped

4 fresh sage leaves

2 garlic cloves, peeled

225g (8oz) Pecorino cheese, finely grated

about 175ml (6fl oz) olive oil

The crisp, salty flavour of the ham blends well with the natural sweetness of the pesto and makes the pork all the more succulent. This recipe is also delicious made with Serrano ham. Be generous when stuffing the pork – a bit of pesto smeared on the outside is fine.

Preheat the oven to 200°C (400°F), gas mark 6. To make the pesto, heat a small heavy-based frying pan over a medium heat. Add the pine nuts and cook until golden brown, tossing occasionally. Tip onto a plate and leave to cool completely. When cool, place in a food processor with the basil, sage, garlic and Pecorino. Blend briefly and then pour in enough of the olive oil to make a thick purée. Blend once more and then season with salt and pepper.

Place one of the pork fillets on a chopping board with the thickest part facing you and ram the handle of a large wooden spoon through its length. Put the pesto in a piping bag fitted with a 2cm (¾in) plain nozzle and pipe into the hole made in the fillet. Alternatively, insert the pesto with a teaspoon. Spread more pesto all over the fillet using a knife, and wrap it in half the ham. If it doesn't stay wrapped together properly, tie it with string at 2.5cm (1in) intervals. Repeat with the second pork fillet and the remaining ingredients.

Place both ham-wrapped pork fillets in a roasting tin and cover with foil. Bake for 15 minutes, then remove the foil and bake for another 5 minutes until the pork is cooked through, the juices run clear when a skewer is inserted, and the ham is crispy. Remove from the oven and leave to rest for 5 minutes in a warm place. Carve the rested pork into slices and arrange on plates with the stuffed tomatoes.

Butterflied Lamb
with Spiced Mint and Yoghurt Rub

2.5kg (5½lb) leg of lamb, boned, butterflied and well trimmed, roughly 5cm (2in) thick

25g (1oz) chopped fresh mint

juice of 2 lemons

4 garlic cloves, peeled and crushed

2 tbsp ground coriander

1 tbsp mild chilli powder

2 tsp ground cumin

4 tbsp extra-virgin olive oil

6 tbsp Greek yoghurt

salt and freshly ground black pepper

lightly dressed green salad, to serve

This lamb recipe was inspired by my Indian friend Naseem, who cooked it on a barbecue. I thought it was a wonderful and tasty way of cooking lamb for a big group of people and I couldn't resist going back for seconds and thirds! Ask your butcher to bone and butterfly the meat for you.

Cut slashes in the lamb to allow the marinade to penetrate it and to encourage the meat to flatten out more. Place in a shallow, non-metallic dish. In a bowl, mix together the mint, lemon juice, garlic, ground coriander, chilli powder, ground cumin, olive oil, yoghurt and a teaspoon of freshly ground black pepper. Rub all over the meat, then cover with clingfilm and chill overnight or leave to stand at room temperature for 2–3 hours if time is short.

Preheat the oven to 240°C (475°F), gas mark 9 or light a barbecue. If the lamb has been chilled overnight, bring it back to room temperature. If cooking in the oven, place the lamb, cut-side up, on a rack in a large roasting tin and season with salt. For rare meat, roast for 25–30 minutes. For medium-rare meat, roast for 35–40 minutes, turning over half way through. If barbecuing, cook over medium–hot coals for about 50 minutes, turning occasionally.

Remove the lamb from the oven or barbecue and leave to rest in a warm place for 10 minutes. If you don't like your lamb too pink, you can cover it with foil at this point and it will continue to cook. Carve into slices and arrange on plates, drizzling over any juices from the tin. Serve with some lightly dressed green salad.

Lamb Rogan Josh

Serves 4

If you're stuck for time, replace the ground spices with four tablespoons of ready-made rogan josh curry paste. This curry tastes even better if the lamb is left to marinate in the sauce for a couple of days before eating. I like to serve this with pilau rice, a dollop of mango chutney and plenty of warm naan bread.

Heat 2 tablespoons of the oil in a large, heavy-based saucepan, add half of the lamb and fry until nicely browned all over. Transfer to a plate and fry the rest of the meat. Set aside.

Add the remaining oil to the pan, then fry the cloves, cinnamon and bay leaves for a few seconds. Add the onion and fry for 6–7 minutes until nicely browned. Add the ginger and garlic and fry for 2 minutes, then add the ground spices and fry for another minute. Add the yoghurt, a tablespoon at a time, cooking for about 30 seconds between each addition.

Return the lamb to the pan and stir in the tomatoes with 150ml (5fl oz) of boiling water. Season to taste, partially cover with a lid, and simmer very gently for about 1 hour or until the lamb is meltingly tender but still holding its shape and the sauce has reduced and thickened.

Spoon the lamb rogan josh onto warmed plates with the rice. Have warm naan breads and mango chutney to hand around separately.

3 tbsp sunflower oil

675g (1½lb) lamb neck fillet, cut into bite-sized pieces

6 whole cloves

1 small cinnamon stick

2 bay leaves

1 large onion, peeled and chopped

5cm (2in) piece of fresh root ginger, peeled and finely grated

4 garlic cloves, peeled and crushed

1 tbsp ground coriander

2 tsp ground cumin

1½ tsp paprika

1 tsp cayenne pepper

¼ tsp ground cardamom

200ml (7fl oz) Greek yoghurt

400g can of chopped tomatoes

salt and freshly ground black pepper

basmati rice, warm naan bread and mango chutney, to serve

Rack of Lamb
with Tapenade Toasts and Wilted Spinach

Serves 4

2 tbsp olive oil

small bunch of fresh mixed herbs (such as basil, mint and flat-leaf parsley)

50g (2oz) fresh white breadcrumbs

2 x 8-bone racks of lamb, each about 275–350g (10–12oz), skinned, chined and French trimmed (ask your butcher to do this)

2 tsp Dijon mustard

1 small baguette, cut into 12 diagonal slices (ends discarded)

salt and freshly ground black pepper

For the red wine sauce

2 tbsp red wine vinegar

300ml (10fl oz) red wine

2 tsp light muscovado sugar

300ml (10fl oz) beef stock (see page 212)

1 tbsp chopped fresh thyme

For the tapenade

250g (9oz) pitted black olives, chopped

juice of 1 lemon

3 tbsp capers, drained

6 anchovy fillets, chopped

1 garlic clove, peeled

2 tbsp chopped fresh flat-leaf parsley

about 120ml (4fl oz) extra-virgin olive oil

A rack of lamb can be expensive as it's the most tender cut, but it is worth every penny. Ask your butcher to 'French trim' the racks of lamb for you, which involves removing the meat and fat from the ribs leaving 5–6cm (2–2½in) of clean bone exposed. This dish can then be prepared well in advance, ready for when your guests arrive.

Preheat the oven to 190°C (375°F), gas mark 5. Put the olive oil, fresh herbs and breadcrumbs in a food processor and blend until you have achieved bright green crumbs.

Prepare the lamb as described, if not already done by the butcher. Place the racks of lamb on a chopping board and, using a pastry brush, spread the mustard thickly over the fat side of each rack. Cover with the herb crumbs and use your hands to mould this crust over the lamb. Cover the tips of the bones with kitchen foil to prevent them burning. Arrange the lamb, coated-side up in a small roasting tin and roast for 15–20 minutes, or a little longer, depending on how pink you like your meat.

Meanwhile, make the red wine sauce. Put a large, heavy-based saucepan over a medium heat and pour in the vinegar and red wine. Simmer for about 5 minutes or until reduced by half. Add the sugar, stock and thyme, and continue to reduce for another 5–10 minutes until the sauce has thickened and coats the back of a spoon without running off. Pass through a sieve, season with salt and pepper and keep warm.

To make the tapenade, place the chopped olives in a food processor with the lemon juice, capers, anchovy fillets, garlic and parsley. Pulse until just combined, then pour in enough olive oil to make a smooth purée. Season to taste and use as required. This will keep well in a sterilised jar in the fridge for up to 1 week.

Remove the lamb from the oven (leaving the oven turned on) and set aside in a warm place to rest for 10–15 minutes. Put the slices of bread on a baking sheet and place in the oven for 3–4 minutes to crisp up.

Meanwhile, prepare the spinach. Remove any large stalks, then wash the leaves and dry well – use a salad spinner if you have one. Heat a large, heavy-based saucepan until very hot and add fistfuls of the spinach, adding another as one wilts down. Cook for 1 minute, then tip into a colander and gently press out the excess moisture.

Melt the butter in the pan set over a medium heat. Skewer the garlic clove on the end of a fork and swirl it in the butter for 30 seconds, then remove. Add the drained spinach and sprinkle with salt, pepper and a little nutmeg. Toss until heated through.

Carve the lamb into individual chops. Divide the spinach among warmed plates and arrange the lamb chops on top, then drizzle around a little of the red wine sauce. The rest can be served in a jug on the table. Spread the toasts with tapenade and arrange around the edge of the plates to serve.

For the wilted spinach
900g (2lb) fresh spinach
25g (1oz) butter
1 garlic clove
pinch of freshly grated nutmeg
salt and freshly ground black pepper

Porchetta with Sautéed Potatoes

4kg (9lb) boneless shoulder of pork with rind

10 long fresh rosemary sprigs

6 garlic cloves, peeled and finely chopped

6 tbsp chopped fresh flat-leaf parsley

75g (3oz) Parmesan cheese, freshly grated

coarse sea salt and freshly ground black pepper

For the sautéed potatoes

1.4kg (3lb) small new potatoes, well scrubbed

175ml (6fl oz) olive oil

8 garlic cloves, peeled and lightly smashed

coarse sea salt and freshly ground black pepper

There is nothing better than gathering the whole family around the table for a leisurely Sunday roast. This classic Italian pork dish is traditionally served on special occasions and at Christmas. I find that a shoulder of pork has just the right balance of meat and fat.

Put the pork on a clean surface, cut loose any butchers strings and open out. Roughly chop the the leaves from three rosemary sprigs and sprinkle over the pork. Sprinkle also with the garlic, parsley and Parmesan and season generously with salt and pepper. Roll the pork back up tightly to enclose the filling completely.

Tie with string at 2cm (¾in) intervals to keep the meat in shape. If the skin is not already scored, use a small sharp knife to score between the strings. Sprinkle with salt, then slip the remaining rosemary sprigs under the strings.

If you prefer the soft, chewy skin which is traditional for this dish, preheat the oven to 190°C (375°F), gas mark 5 and roast the pork straight away for 20 minutes per 500g (1lb 2oz), plus 20 minutes. For example, if your joint is exactly 4kg (9lb), it will take 3 hours. If you want a crunchy crackling (this makes it harder to carve), leave at room temperature for at least 2 hours and dab away excess water with kitchen paper before roasting. Cook as above, but turn up the oven to 220°C (425°F), gas mark 7 for the last 20 minutes of cooking time.

Remove from the oven and leave to rest for a good 30 minutes, as porchetta is best served warm rather than piping hot.

To sauté the potatoes, first cook in boiling salted water for 10–15 minutes until tender, then drain. Heat the olive oil in a large frying pan set over a fairly high heat and add the garlic, followed by the potatoes. Allow to brown on all sides, stirring now and again to prevent them sticking to the pan. Season with salt and pepper.

Carve the porchetta into thin slices (an electric carving knife is useful) and arrange on warmed plates with the sautéed potatoes.

Vietnamese Beef Noodle Soup
(Pho Bo)

Serves 4

Pho is the national food of Vietnam, where it is normally eaten for lunch and can be bought from street vendors. It usually comes with a plateful of herbs such as Asian basil and mint, bean sprouts and green chillies, which diners add according to their own taste. Pho is wonderfully fresh and light and takes me right back to the streets of Saigon.

Pour the stock into a large saucepan and add the ginger, star anise, if using, and the cinnamon. Bring to the boil, then reduce the heat and simmer for 15 minutes.

Meanwhile, using a very sharp knife, cut the sirloin across the grain into very thin strips. Set aside.

Put the noodles in a large bowl with enough boiling water to cover them. Soak for 15 minutes or until softened and pliable. Drain the noodles in a colander, then place in a pan of boiling water and simmer for 45 seconds until tender or according to the packet instructions. Drain well and set aside.

Strain the flavoured stock into a clean saucepan and heat to a simmer. Stir in the Thai fish sauce and the black pepper. Add the sliced sirloin steak and simmer for 30–45 seconds or until the meat loses its redness. Skim off any froth from the soup.

To serve, divide the noodles between four warmed large bowls and place a pile of the beansprouts on top of each one. Ladle over the flavoured beef broth and sprinkle the spring onions, coriander, chillies, basil and mint on top. Garnish with the lime wedges to serve.

1.2 litres (2 pints) beef stock (see page 212)

2.5cm (1in) piece of fresh root ginger, peeled and sliced

2 whole star anise (optional)

1 cinnamon stick

225g (8oz) boneless beef sirloin, trimmed of any fat and slightly frozen

225g (8oz) dried flat rice noodles (*banh pho*)

3 tbsp Thai fish sauce (*nam pla*)

100g (4oz) fresh bean sprouts, rinsed and drained

4 spring onions, trimmed and finely chopped

small bunch of fresh coriander, leaves stripped and finely chopped

2 red or green Thai bird's eye chillies, thinly sliced

handful of fresh basil and mint leaves, torn

good pinch of freshly ground black pepper

lime wedges, to garnish

fish and shellfish

Black Cod with a Sweet Basil Crust
and Roasted Vine Tomatoes

Serves 4

150g (5oz) slightly stale brioche or white bread, cut into cubes

good handful of fresh basil leaves

75g (3oz) butter

finely grated rind of 1 orange

pinch of freshly grated nutmeg

4 x 175g (6oz) black cod fillets, skin left on, pin bones removed

1 egg yolk, lightly beaten

4 cherry tomato vines, each with 5–7 tomatoes

1 tbsp olive oil

Maldon sea salt and freshly ground black pepper

baby new potatoes, boiled and buttered, and a lightly dressed green salad, to serve

Despite the name, black cod is actually unrelated to regular cod. It is fished in southern and sub-Antarctic waters and is a good sustainable alternative. Ensure you leave the skin on as the flesh has a tendency to break up while cooking. The sweet basil crust will also work nicely on haddock, monkfish or salmon.

Preheat the oven to 200ºC (400ºF), gas mark 6. Whiz the brioche or bread with the basil in a food processor to make vibrant green breadcrumbs.

Heat the butter in a small saucepan set over a medium heat until just melted, then stir in the orange rind and nutmeg. Remove from the heat and stir in the green breadcrumbs, then tip onto a plate. Leave to cool.

Rub the flesh of the cod fillets with salt and pepper and arrange skin-side down on a baking tray lined with non-stick parchment paper.

Brush the top of the cod fillets with the beaten egg yolk, then press the flavoured crumbs down on top. Arrange the tomatoes around the edge of the fish, drizzle over the olive oil and sprinkle with salt and pepper. Bake for 15–20 minutes until the cod is cooked through, the crust is crisp and lightly golden, and the tomatoes are tender and their skins have split.

Arrange the cooked black cod on warmed plates with the roasted vine tomatoes. Put bowls of buttered boiled potatoes and green salad on the table to hand around separately.

Mackerel
with Puy Lentils and Sherry Vinaigrette

Serves 4

Mackerel is an under-used fish that is in plentiful supply. Naturally rich in oil and low in saturated fat, it is full of vitamins and minerals, and an excellent source of essential omega 3 fats. The body needs a regular supply of omega 3, so try to eat oil-rich fish, like mackerel, salmon or trout, at least once a week.

Rinse the lentils under plenty of cold running water and place in a saucepan, cover with water and bring to the boil. Add a good pinch of salt and simmer for 25 minutes or until the lentils are just tender but still holding their shape.

Meanwhile, make the sherry vinaigrette. Place the vinegar in a screw-top jar with the olive oil, golden syrup, mustard and sugar. Add seasoning, then screw the lid on tightly and shake vigorously until well combined. Set aside until needed.

Drain the cooked lentils, then return to the pan and place over a low heat. Add the carrot, onion and enough stock to cover the lentils and cook for about 10 minutes or until the lentils have absorbed all the stock. Add the sugar, vinegar and tomato purée, and stir to combine. Season with salt and pepper and keep warm.

Heat the olive oil in a non-stick frying pan. Season the mackerel fillets with salt and pepper and, using a small knife, make small incisions in the skin to prevent the fish from curling up. Put the fillets in the heated pan and cook for 5–7 minutes, turning once, until the skin is crisp and the mackerel is cooked through.

To serve, stir the chives into the Puy lentils, heap onto the centre of warmed plates and place the mackerel fillets on top. Drizzle the sherry vinaigrette around the plates and garnish with rocket.

200g (7oz) Puy lentils, soaked overnight

2 tbsp finely chopped carrot

2 tbsp finely chopped onion

350ml (12fl oz) beef or chicken stock (see pages 212 and 215)

2 tsp sugar

2 tsp balsamic vinegar

2 tsp tomato purée

1 tbsp snipped fresh chives

2 tbsp olive oil

8 medium mackerel fillets, skin left on, pin bones removed

salt and freshly ground black pepper

25g (1oz) wild rocket, to garnish

For the sherry vinaigrette

2 tbsp sherry vinegar

4 tbsp extra-virgin olive oil

1 tsp golden syrup

1 tsp wholegrain mustard

pinch of light muscovado sugar

salt and freshly ground black pepper

Seared Scallops
with Date Jam and Curried Cauliflower Purée

Serves 6

18 large sea scallops, well trimmed

1 tsp olive oil

salt

For the date jam

225g (8oz) Medjool dates, pitted

2 tbsp crème de cassis

2 tsp balsamic vinegar

2 tbsp light muscovado sugar

For the cauliflower purée

1 small cauliflower

25g (1oz) butter

1 tsp mild curry powder

100ml (3½fl oz) milk

100ml (3½fl oz) single cream

Maldon sea salt and freshly ground black pepper

about 6 tbsp Five-spice Balsamic Cream, to garnish (see page 217)

This is one of my most successful scallop recipes – it's been on the menu in my restaurant for years. Its success is down to the combination of three things – the sweetness of the scallops, the fragrant cauliflower purée and the slight taste of toffee from the date jam. It is worth seeking out Medjool dates grown in Egypt or California. Their slightly wrinkled skin encases a dense, sweet flesh.

To make the date jam, place 300ml (10fl oz) of water in a pan with the dates. Set over a medium heat, bring to a simmer and cook gently for 10–15 minutes until the dates are completely soft and the liquid is slightly reduced. Stir in the crème de cassis, vinegar and sugar and cook for another minute or so until the sugar has dissolved. Leave to cool, then blend in a food processor until smooth. Transfer to a bowl and cover with clingfilm until needed.

To make the cauliflower purée, cut the cauliflower into small florets, discarding the leaves and stalk. Melt the butter in a saucepan with a lid and stir in the curry powder. Add the florets and cook over a medium heat for 3 minutes, stirring regularly, until just beginning to soften. Add the milk and cream, cover and simmer for another 8 minutes or until the cauliflower is completely soft and the milk mixture is slightly reduced. Place in a food processor or use a hand-held blender and whiz to a smooth purée. Pass through a sieve into a bowl. Season with salt and pepper and either leave to cool completely, then cover with clingfilm in the fridge until needed or, if using immediately, keep warm.

To cook the scallops, heat the olive oil in a non-stick frying pan set over a very high heat. Season the scallops with some salt, then quickly sear them for about 1 minute on each side until golden brown and nicely caramelised. They should still be slightly undercooked in the middle. You may need to do this in batches, depending on the size of your pan. ◗

Warm the Five-spice Balsamic Cream in a small saucepan. Spoon some of the cauliflower purée onto each warmed plate and arrange three scallops on each. Add a spoonful of date jam and drizzle with a little of the balsamic cream to serve.

Baked Sea Bass
with Tomatoes and Olives

Serves 4

4 x 275g (10oz) whole sea bass, scaled and gutted

8 fresh bay leaves

4 firm plum tomatoes, thinly sliced

1 lime, sliced

100g (4oz) pitted black olives, sliced

4 garlic cloves, peeled and sliced

2 tbsp roughly chopped fresh fennel herb

handful of fresh basil leaves

4 tbsp olive oil, plus extra for greasing

salt and freshly ground black pepper

boiled baby new potatoes and lightly dressed green salad, to serve

The chances are that any good fishmonger will have a plentiful supply of farmed sea bass. It is great value for money and has a good flavour. This is a glamorous and colourful dish that would work just as well with grey mullet.

Preheat the oven to 190°C (375°F), gas mark 5. Using a sharp knife, cut the heads and tails off the sea bass (or get your fishmonger to do this for you). Make two narrow slashes in each fish, cutting about half way down, and insert a bay leaf into each incision.

Place the sea bass in a large, lightly greased roasting tin. Season inside the fish cavities with salt and pepper, then fill each fish with tomatoes, half the lime slices, the olives, garlic, fennel and basil leaves. Drizzle over the olive oil and season the fish a little more.

Roast the sea bass for 15–20 minutes until the skin is crisp and the flesh is just cooked through and tender. When the fish is cooked, the flesh will feel firm and the dorsal fin (the large one on the back) will come away when pulled. Allow the fish to rest for 2–3 minutes, then transfer to warmed plates. Arrange the remaining slices of lime on the fish and serve with separate bowls of baby new potatoes and green salad.

Grilled Salmon
with Avocado and Sun-dried Tomato Dressing

Serves 6

Organic salmon is best to use for this dish because it is farmed in colder waters and so has a firmer flesh. Salmon tastes far better when slightly underdone than it does when overcooked, so ensure it doesn't cook for too long and serve it warm rather than piping hot.

To make the dressing, place the sun-dried tomatoes in a food processor with the olive oil, lemon juice, chilli powder and basil leaves. Blend together for about 1 minute until you have achieved a fairly smooth texture. Season with salt and pepper and transfer to a jug.

Cut each salmon fillet into three pieces. Heat a griddle or frying pan until smoking hot. Season the salmon pieces and brush each one with a little olive oil, then place on the griddle pan. Reduce the heat and cook for 3–4 minutes on each side until just cooked through and golden brown. Remove the salmon from the heat and splash with the lemon juice.

To serve, cut the avocados in half and remove the stones, then carefully peel off the skin. Cut each half into three wedges and divide among serving plates. Place pieces of salmon between the wedges of avocado and drizzle a little of the dressing over the plates. Pile the rocket into the centre of each plate and drizzle over some more of the dressing.

6 x 175g (6oz) skinless salmon fillets, pin bones removed

olive oil, for brushing

juice of ½ lemon

3 ripe avocados

salt and freshly ground black pepper

25g (1oz) wild rocket, to serve

For the dressing

12 sun blushed tomatoes in oil, drained

200ml (7fl oz) olive oil

1 tsp fresh lemon juice

pinch of chilli powder

3 fresh basil leaves

salt and freshly ground black pepper

Fried Butterflied Sardines
with Aubergine Chutney

Serves 4

40g (1½oz) Parmesan cheese, freshly grated

1 tbsp chopped fresh flat-leaf parsley

200g (7oz) fresh white breadcrumbs

75g (3oz) plain flour

2 eggs, beaten

a little milk

12 sardines, scaled and butterflied (ask your fishmonger to do this)

sunflower oil, for deep-frying

salt and freshly ground black pepper

lightly dressed wild rocket salad (optional), to serve

For the chutney

4 tbsp olive oil

1 large aubergine, cut into 1cm (½in) dice

1 onion, peeled and finely chopped

1 celery stick, finely chopped

2.5cm (1in) piece of fresh root ginger, peeled and finely chopped

1 tsp medium curry powder

1 tbsp tomato purée

2 tbsp light muscovado sugar

2 tbsp red wine vinegar

50g (2oz) pine nuts

50g (2oz) raisins

4 tbsp roughly chopped fresh coriander

salt and freshly ground black pepper

These sardines need to be butterflied, with their heads removed and most of the backbone taken out, leaving just an inch at the tail end. Ask your fishmonger to do this for you. Leftover chutney will keep for 3–4 days in a sealed container in the fridge – it's great with a cheese sandwich!

To make the chutney, heat the olive oil in a large frying pan. Add the aubergine, season with salt and pepper and sauté for 8–10 minutes until cooked through and tender. Add the onion, celery and ginger and cook for another 4–5 minutes until the vegetables are softened but not browned.

Sprinkle the curry powder over the aubergine mixture, add the tomato purée and cook for 2–3 minutes, stirring. Add the sugar, vinegar and 6 tablespoons of water, stir to combine, then simmer gently for another 5 minutes until well reduced and thickened.

Meanwhile, heat a frying pan over a medium heat and toast the pine nuts, tossing occasionally. Add to the aubergine mixture with the raisins and coriander, season to taste and simmer gently for another 5 minutes to allow the flavours to combine and until the coriander has wilted. Transfer to a bowl and set aside to cool.

Mix the Parmesan, parsley and breadcrumbs in a shallow dish. Place the flour on a flat plate and season generously. Lightly beat the eggs and milk in a bowl. Dip the butterflied sardines into the seasoned flour, shake off any excess, then coat in the beaten egg. Finally, roll them in the breadcrumb mixture, pressing it on well to give an even coating. Chill until ready to cook.

Pour the oil into a large, heavy-based saucepan or heat a deep-fat fryer to 180°C (350°F) – a small piece of white bread dropped into the oil should brown and rise to the surface in about 1 minute. Fry the sardines for 1 minute, flipping over half way through to brown both sides. Lift out with a slotted spoon and drain well on kitchen paper. To serve, arrange on warmed plates with small mounds of the aubergine chutney. Garnish with the rocket salad, if using.

Seared Tuna
with Sweetcorn, Red Pepper and Lime Salsa

Serves 4

Tuna is always a good buy as there is very little waste. It is best eaten seared on the outside but slightly undercooked in the middle. A cast-iron griddle pan is the ideal utensil for cooking this dish, although a barbecue imparts a superior flavour.

4 x 175g (6oz) tuna loin fillets

2 tbsp olive oil

salt and freshly ground black pepper

lightly dressed green salad, to serve

For the salsa

1 fresh cob of sweetcorn

1 red pepper

1 tbsp chilli oil (see page 219 or shop-bought)

1 garlic clove, peeled and crushed

1 medium-hot red chilli, seeded and finely chopped

finely grated rind and juice of 1 lime

1 tbsp chopped fresh mixed herbs (such as coriander and flat-leaf parsley)

salt and freshly ground black pepper

To make the salsa, bring a saucepan of water to the boil and cook the sweetcorn for 6–8 minutes until tender, then drain well and leave to cool. Using a sharp knife, cut off the kernels and place them in a bowl. Set aside until needed.

You can roast the pepper in one of several ways. Spear the stalk end of the pepper on a fork and hold over the flame of a gas hob, turning regularly until the skin has blistered and blackened. Alternatively, scorch with a chef's blow torch or preheat the oven to 220°C (425°F), gas mark 7 and roast in a small tin for 20–25 minutes until the skin is black. Put the blackened pepper in a plastic food bag, seal and leave to cool completely. Once cool, cut in half and discard the stalk, skin and seeds. Cut the flesh into small dice and add to the bowl with the sweetcorn kernels.

Put the chilli oil, garlic and red chilli into a small saucepan, heat gently and as soon as the liquid starts to sizzle, pour onto the sweetcorn and pepper dice, mixing well to combine. Add the lime rind and juice along with the herbs and season the salsa with salt and pepper.

Heat a griddle pan or heavy-based frying pan over a high heat until very hot. Brush the tuna fillets all over with olive oil, sprinkle with salt and pepper and add to the pan. Cook for 2 minutes on each side if you like your tuna still a little rare in the middle, or cook for a few minutes longer if you prefer it more well done.

Arrange the seared tuna fillets on warmed serving plates and spoon some of the salsa alongside, placing the remainder in a bowl on the table. Serve with a lightly dressed green salad.

Smoked Fish Platter
with Smoked Salmon Brandade

Serves 4–6

100g (4oz) smoked trout fillets

100g (4oz) smoked mackerel fillets, skin removed

100g (4oz) smoked eel fillets

lemon wedges and sliced brown soda bread or bruschetta (see page 17), to serve

fresh chives, to garnish

For the brandade

175g (6oz) floury potatoes, peeled and cut into chunks

200ml (7fl oz) milk

2 garlic cloves, peeled and crushed

100ml (3½fl oz) olive oil, plus extra for drizzling

350g (12oz) smoked salmon slices

1 tsp fresh lemon juice

1 tsp chopped fresh flat-leaf parsley

salt and freshly ground black pepper

This is an excellent way to get your weekly intake of oily fish and omega 3. It will only be as good as the ingredients you choose, so you could try visting a smoke house to buy really good-quality smoked fish. Brandade is traditionally made with salt cod, but smoked salmon makes a delicious variation.

To prepare the brandade, cook the potatoes in a saucepan of boiling salted water for 15–20 minutes or until cooked through and tender. Drain and keep warm.

Place the milk, garlic and olive oil in another saucepan and gently warm through, then remove from the heat. Place the smoked salmon in a food processor and, with the motor running, slowly add small amounts of the milk mixture until you have a thick, wet paste.

Add the cooked potatoes to the smoked salmon mixture in the food processor and pulse until just combined. Be careful not to overmix at this stage. Transfer the brandade to a bowl and stir in the lemon juice and parsley. Season with black pepper.

Place the bowl of smoked salmon brandade on a large platter and arrange the smoked trout, smoked mackerel and smoked eel around it. Garnish with lemon wedges and serve with a separate bowl of sliced brown soda bread or bruschetta.

Roasted Haddock

with Smoked Bacon, Haricot Bean Purée and Wilted Spinach

Serves 4

2 tbsp olive oil

4 x 175g (6oz) haddock fillets, skin on and boned

25g (1oz) butter, diced

100g (4oz) piece of smoked bacon, rind removed and diced

1 tbsp chopped fresh flat-leaf parsley

good squeeze of lemon juice

salt and freshly ground black pepper

For the haricot bean purée

2 tbsp extra-virgin olive oil

25g (1oz) unsalted butter

1 large onion, peeled and finely chopped

2 garlic cloves, peeled and crushed

400g can of haricot beans, drained and rinsed

For the spinach

900g (2lb) fresh spinach

25g (1oz) butter

1 garlic clove, peeled and crushed (optional)

pinch of freshly grated nutmeg

This haddock is served with haricot bean purée, an excellent alternative to mash and a great store-cupboard standby. It is also good served with roasted vine tomatoes (see page 181).

To make the haricot bean purée, place the extra-virgin olive oil and unsalted butter in a heavy-based pan over a gentle heat. Add the onion and garlic and cook for about 10 minutes until softened but not browned. Stir in the haricot beans and continue to cook for a few minutes until heated through, then whiz to a purée using a hand-held blender. Season with salt and pepper and keep warm.

Meanwhile, heat 1 tablespoon of olive oil in a heavy-based frying pan and add the haddock fillets, skin-side down. Fry for a minute or two until the skin just begins to crisp up, then add small knobs of butter around each fillet and continue to cook for another minute or so until nicely crisp. Turn the fish over and fry for 3–4 minutes more until cooked through. Cooking time will depend on the thickness of the fillets. Transfer the cooked fish to a warm plate and keep warm while you make the bacon dressing.

Add the remaining tablespoon of olive oil to the frying pan and tip in the smoked bacon. Sauté for 3–4 minutes until sizzling and the bacon has begun to release some oil. Remove from the heat and add the parsley and lemon juice. Swirl the pan until the dressing is nicely combined and then season with salt and pepper.

To prepare the spinach, remove any large stalks, then wash and dry well – use a salad spinner if you have one. Heat a large, heavy-based saucepan and add fistfuls of the spinach, adding another as each one wilts down. Cook for 1 minute, then tip into a colander and gently press out all the excess moisture.

Melt the remaining butter in the pan and sauté the garlic for 30 seconds, if using, then add the drained spinach, and season with salt and pepper and a little nutmeg. Toss until heated through.

Arrange mounds of haricot bean purée on warmed plates and top each with a piece of haddock, skin-side up. Drizzle with the bacon dressing and serve with a separate bowl of the wilted spinach.

Hake with Clams, Fennel and Cherry Tomatoes
in Parchment Paper

Serves 4

4 tbsp extra-virgin olive oil

50g (2oz) raw chorizo sausage, skinned and diced

2 garlic cloves, peeled and sliced

225g (8oz) cherry tomatoes

1 tsp caster sugar

½ tsp smoked paprika

1 tsp chopped fresh fennel or dill

4 x 150g (5oz) skinless hake fillets, pin bones removed

20 large clams (such as *palourde*), scrubbed

4 tbsp fino dry sherry

4 slices of sourdough bread

1 tbsp Dijon mustard

1 tbsp fresh lemon juice

4 tbsp light olive oil

150g (5oz) wild rocket

Maldon sea salt and freshly ground black pepper

This must be one of the healthiest ways to cook fish. It's vital not to overcook the fish – when the parcels are opened and the hake gently pressed, it should give slightly, but not too much. If it's wobbly or jelly-like, then it is undercooked. Many types of clams are now available but my favourite are *palourde*.

Preheat the oven to 200°C (400°F), gas mark 6. Place a large baking sheet in the oven to preheat.

Heat 1 tablespoon of extra-virgin olive oil in a heavy-based frying pan over a high heat. Add the chorizo and sauté for 2–3 minutes until sizzling. Stir in the garlic and cook until soft, then tip in the tomatoes with the sugar and paprika. Sauté for 3–4 minutes until the tomatoes have just begun to split, then remove from the heat. Stir in the fennel or dill and season with salt and pepper.

Cut the largest circle possible from non-stick parchment paper. Repeat to create four circles in total. Divide the tomato mixture between them, placing it in the centre of the paper. Put a fillet of hake on top of each one, followed by five clams and a tablespoon of sherry. Drizzle half a tablespoon of extra-virgin olive oil over each piece of fish and sprinkle with salt and pepper. Bring the two sides of each circle together and fold over to form a loose parcel.

Place the parcels on the baking sheet and put in the oven for 6–8 minutes until the hake is cooked and the clams have opened; discard any that remain closed.

Meanwhile, heat a griddle pan until very hot. Toast the sourdough for about 1 minute on each side, until lightly charred. Drizzle with the remaining extra-virgin olive oil and sprinkle with sea salt.

To make a dressing, whisk the mustard with the lemon juice in a small bowl, then slowly add the light olive oil and whisk until smooth. Season with salt and pepper. Place the rocket in another bowl and pour over enough dressing to lightly coat the leaves.

To serve, place a fish parcel onto a warmed plate. Serve with a lightly dressed salad and a piece of grilled sourdough bread.

Seared Swordfish
with Salsa Verde

Serves 4

Swordfish is very meaty and goes well with the clean, sharp taste of salsa verde. The salsa is best used while fresh, although it will keep for 2–3 days in the fridge.

To make the salsa, mix together the parsley, basil and mint with the garlic, capers and anchovy fillets and chop them all coarsely or pulse in a food processor – although you do get a better, chunkier result if you chop by hand.

Transfer to a non-metallic bowl and gradually whisk in the red wine vinegar, lemon juice and Dijon mustard with the olive oil. Season with half a teaspoon of salt and a quarter teaspoon of pepper. These quantities should make about 225ml (8fl oz) of salsa in total. Cover with clingfilm, and set aside at room temperature.

Heat a griddle pan or heavy-based frying pan and brush with the olive oil, then add the swordfish steaks and fry for 3 minutes on each side until cooked through and lightly charred. Transfer the swordfish steaks to a plate, season with salt and set aside in a warm place for about 5 minutes.

To serve, arrange the swordfish steaks on warmed plates and spoon some of the salsa verde to the side. Serve at once with a separate bowl of boiled new potatoes.

1 tbsp extra-virgin olive oil

4 x 175g (6oz) swordfish steaks

Maldon sea salt and freshly ground black pepper

boiled new potatoes, to serve

For the salsa verde

2 handfuls of fresh flat-leaf parsley

12 fresh basil leaves

1 small handful of fresh mint leaves

2 garlic cloves, peeled

2 tbsp capers, drained and rinsed

4 anchovy fillets, drained

1 tbsp red wine vinegar

1 tbsp fresh lemon juice

1 tbsp Dijon mustard

6 tbsp extra-virgin olive oil

Monkfish
in Thai Yellow Curry Broth

Serves 4

900g (2lb) skinless monkfish fillets, cut into bite-sized cubes

fresh coriander leaves, to garnish

jasmine rice, to serve

For the yellow curry broth

2 shallots, peeled and chopped

2cm (¾in) piece of fresh root ginger or galangal, peeled and finely chopped

1 lemongrass stalk, outer leaves removed and finely chopped

grated rind and juice of 1 lime

1 tbsp Thai fish sauce (*nam pla*) or light soy sauce

2 yellow or green chillies, thinly sliced, plus extra to garnish

2 garlic cloves, peeled and crushed

2 spring onions, thinly sliced, plus extra to garnish

1 tsp ground coriander

1 tsp mustard seeds

½ tsp ground turmeric

400ml can of coconut milk

600ml (1 pint) vegetable or chicken stock (see pages 213 and 215)

salt and freshly ground black pepper

This curry is beautifully fragrant and much more refreshing than traditional hearty fish stews – perfect for a summer evening. If you fancy a change from monkfish, you could use calamari instead; just reduce the cooking time by a couple of minutes to prevent it from going rubbery.

To make a yellow curry paste, place the shallots in a mini blender with the ginger, lemongrass, lime rind and juice, Thai fish sauce or soy sauce, chillies, garlic, spring onions, coriander, mustard seeds and turmeric. Blend with enough of the coconut milk to form a paste. If you don't have a mini blender, use a pestle and mortar to crush the ingredients or chop them very finely with a large knife and then stir into the coconut milk.

Transfer the yellow curry paste to a large saucepan with a lid and cook over a medium heat for 1 minute, stirring. Pour in the stock and the rest of the coconut milk, turn up the heat and bring to the boil, then reduce the heat and simmer for 5 minutes until fragrant. Season generously with salt and pepper.

Add the monkfish to the pan and simmer gently for another 3–4 minutes until the fish is just tender but still holding its shape. Ladle the monkfish and broth into large, wide-rimmed serving bowls and garnish with the coriander leaves, yellow chillies and spring onions. Serve at once with individual bowls of the jasmine rice.

Crispy Lemon Sole
with Chilli Jam and Curried Mayonnaise

Serves 6

This lemon sole is delicious with chilli jam, one of my store-cupboard essentials. The jam is simple to make and freezes well. You could also try it drizzled over grilled Mediterranean vegetables or with grilled goat's cheese.

To make the chilli jam, heat the olive oil in a heavy-based saucepan set over a low heat and sweat the peppers, onions and garlic for 2 minutes. Add the chilli and tomato purée and simmer for 3 minutes. Then add the vinegar, sugar, tomatoes and soy sauce, and stir to combine. Pour in enough water to just cover the ingredients, mix well to combine, then simmer for 15–20 minutes, stirring occasionally, until slightly reduced and thickened. Leave to cool.

Once the mixture has cooled, place in a food processor and blend to a purée, then pass through a sieve and season with salt and pepper. Transfer to a squeezy plastic bottle and set aside until needed. This can be refrigerated or frozen for up to one week.

Place the mayonnaise in a bowl and beat in the curry paste, lemon juice and chives. Season with salt and pepper, cover with clingfilm and chill until needed.

Put the sunflower oil in a wok or heavy-based saucepan and turn the heat right up, or heat a deep-fat fryer to 180ºC (350ºF). Whisk together the egg whites and cream in a shallow bowl and set aside. Place the flour, sesame seeds, chilli powder and curry powder in a separate shallow bowl, add a large pinch of white pepper and half a teaspoon of salt. Stir until well combined.

Dip one piece of sole at a time into the egg mixture, coating well and gently shaking off any excess. Then dip the fish pieces into the spiced flour until evenly coated. Deep-fry for about 2 minutes or until golden and crispy. You may have to do this in batches. Remove from the oil and drain well on kitchen paper.

Arrange the crispy lemon sole on warmed plates. Add a dollop of the curried mayonnaise and garnish each plate with a squiggle of the chilli jam. Serve at once with a separate bowl of green salad.

sunflower oil, for deep-frying

2 egg whites

2 tbsp double cream

150g (5oz) plain flour

3 tbsp sesame seeds

2 tsp chilli powder

2 tsp curry powder

salt and freshly ground white pepper

675g (1½lb) lemon sole fillets, skinned and cut into small pieces on the diagonal

lightly dressed green salad, to serve

For the chilli jam

1 tbsp olive oil

2 red peppers, halved, seeded and diced

2 onions, peeled and diced

1 garlic clove, peeled and crushed

1 red chilli, seeded and finely chopped

1 tbsp tomato purée

1 tbsp balsamic vinegar

50g (2oz) light muscovado sugar

4 ripe tomatoes, diced

splash of dark soy sauce

For the curried mayonnaise

120ml (4fl oz) mayonnaise

2 tsp mild curry paste

juice of ½ lemon

1 tsp snipped fresh chives

vegetables and salads

Gorgonzola, Pear and Rocket Salad

20cm (8in) piece of French baguette (slightly stale if possible)

50g (2oz) Gorgonzola cheese, rind removed

75g (3oz) ricotta cheese

50g (2oz) unsalted butter, at room temperature

1 tbsp snipped fresh chives

1 tsp fresh lemon juice

2 Conference pears (ripe but firm)

25g (1oz) butter

2 tsp caster sugar

100g (4oz) bag of rocket, spinach and watercress salad (or similar)

25g (1oz) shelled walnuts, lightly toasted and coarsely chopped

1½ tsp balsamic vinegar

2 tbsp extra-virgin olive oil

salt and freshly ground black pepper

Very stylish, very simple and very delicious! This is a perfect combination of ingredients, but feel free to substitute Roquefort, Stilton or Cashel Blue for the Gorgonzola if you prefer.

Preheat the oven to 150°C (300°F), gas mark 2. To make some croûtons, cut the baguette on the diagonal into 12 very thin slices, discarding the ends. Arrange on a baking sheet and cook in the oven for 10–15 minutes until crisp and lightly golden.

Meanwhile, place the Gorgonzola in a bowl with the ricotta, unsalted butter, chives and lemon juice. Mash together with a fork until well blended and season generously with pepper.

Peel the pears, then cut into slices, removing the cores. Melt the butter in a small saucepan and scatter in the sugar. Add the pears and gently fry for 4½ minutes, turning, until caramelised. Spread the toasted croûtons thickly with the Gorgonzola mixture and arrange the pear slices in an overlapping layer on top.

Place the salad leaves in a large bowl with the chopped walnuts and splash over the balsamic vinegar. Season generously and lightly dress with the olive oil. Divide the salad leaves between wide-rimmed bowls and arrange three croûtons around the edge of each bowl. Serve at once.

Chunky Greek Salad
with Feta Cheese

Serves 4 | VEGETARIAN

This summer salad conjures up delicious images of tavernas in the warm sun, where it is always served dressed with just olive oil and never with vinaigrette as you may imagine. It is a very transportable feast and needs nothing more than a hunk of crusty bread and a glass of gutsy red wine to make a fine light lunch. You could also serve with Grilled Rib-eye Steak (see page 63) and a homemade infused olive oil (see page 219).

Soak the chopped onion in a bowl of iced water for 5–10 minutes to remove its sharpness. Drain well on kitchen paper.

Place the onion in a serving bowl with the cherry tomatoes and cucumber, then mix gently to combine. Scatter over the feta and olives, then sprinkle over the parsley. Season with salt and pepper and drizzle over the olive oil. Serve at once.

1 red onion, peeled and roughly chopped

225g (8oz) cherry tomatoes, halved

½ cucumber, peeled and cut into chunks

150g (5oz) feta cheese, cut into cubes

handful of good-quality black olives

1 tbsp chopped fresh flat-leaf parsley

3–4 tbsp extra-virgin olive oil (or infused olive oil – page 219)

salt and freshly ground black pepper

Salade Niçoise

4 x 100g (4oz) fresh tuna steaks, each 2.5cm (1in) thick, or 2 x 200g cans of tuna in sunflower oil

8 salad potatoes

4 eggs (preferably free-range or organic), at room temperature

100g (4oz) extra-fine French beans, trimmed

4 little gem lettuce hearts, quartered lengthways and separated into leaves

175g (6oz) cherry tomatoes, halved

1 red onion, peeled and finely sliced

6 anchovy fillets, drained and thinly sliced lengthways

16 pitted black olives in brine, drained

8 fresh basil leaves, torn

For the marinade

7 tbsp extra-virgin olive oil

3 tbsp red wine vinegar

2 tbsp chopped fresh flat-leaf parsley

2 tbsp snipped fresh chives

2 garlic cloves, peeled and finely chopped

salt and freshly ground black pepper

This deliciously informal dish can be as generous as you like, so feel free to experiment with all the quantities. The tuna is best cooked until medium-rare so that it remains moist, but cook for a minute or two longer if you prefer, or just use canned tuna.

Place all the ingredients for the marinade in a bowl, along with a teaspoon each of salt and pepper, and whisk to combine.

Put the tuna steaks in a shallow, non-metallic dish and pour over half of the marinade. Cover with clingfilm and chill for 1–2 hours to allow the flavours to penetrate the tuna, turning every 30 minutes or so.

Bring a medium saucepan of salted water to the boil, add the potatoes and cover and simmer for 10–12 minutes or until just tender. Drain and leave to cool completely, then cut them all in half.

Place the eggs, still in their shells, into a small saucepan of boiling water – enough to just cover them – and cook for 6 minutes. Drain and rinse under cold running water, then peel off the shells and cut each egg into quarters lengthways. Plunge the French beans into a saucepan of boiling salted water for a minute or so, then drain and refresh under cold running water.

Heat a griddle pan or heavy-based frying pan over a very high heat for 5 minutes. Remove the tuna from the marinade, shaking off any excess liquid. Cook the tuna steaks for 2–3 minutes on each side, depending on how rare you want them. Cut into chunks. Arrange the lettuce leaves on serving plates or one large platter and add the potatoes, French beans, tomatoes, onion and anchovies. Place the chunks of tuna on top and drizzle over the remaining marinade. Scatter over the eggs, olives and torn basil leaves to serve.

Pomegranate, Orange and Mint Salad

Serves 4 | VEGETARIAN

This salad makes a refreshing starter on a hot day. It is also perfect served as a side salad with barbecued lamb or roast pork, or between courses as a palate cleanser. Use the sweetest oranges you can find.

To get slices of orange without any bitter pith, remove a slice from the top and bottom of the orange, then, with a very sharp knife, carefully cut away the skin and pith following the curve of the orange, continuing along the orange until you have removed all the peel and pith. Cut the orange into slices and then repeat with the remaining oranges. Reserve any juice for the dressing.

To make the dressing, whisk together the olive oil and orange juice, along with any pomegranate juice, then season lightly with salt and pepper. Arrange the orange slices on a large plate and sprinkle with the pomegranate seeds. Drizzle the dressing over the salad. Roughly tear the mint leaves and scatter on top to serve.

5–6 large oranges (Valencia if available)

seeds (and any juice) of 1 large pomegranate

2 tbsp extra-virgin olive oil (or infused olive oil, see page 219)

6 tbsp fresh orange juice

handful of fresh mint leaves

salt and freshly ground black pepper

Chargrilled Thai Beef Salad

1 tsp jasmine rice

2 dried small red chillies

500g (1lb 2oz) thick beef fillet

2 tbsp toasted sesame oil

5 tbsp *ketjap manis* (sweet soy sauce)

1 small cucumber, peeled, halved, seeded and cut into 1cm (½in) slices

4 red shallots, peeled and thinly sliced

100g (4oz) cherry tomatoes, halved

1 mild red chilli, seeded and thinly sliced

handful of fresh mint leaves

handful of fresh coriander leaves

small handful of fresh basil leaves, torn

4 spring onions, trimmed and thinly sliced

2 tsp caster sugar

4 tbsp fresh lime juice

3 tbsp Thai fish sauce (*nam pla*)

100g (4oz) mixed green salad leaves

The people of Thailand and neighbouring countries are very fond of this salad. This is an authentic recipe that I picked up on my travels and have enjoyed cooking once back at home. It's also very good with prawns.

If using a charcoal barbecue to grill the beef, light it 30 minutes before you want to start cooking. If using a gas barbecue, light it 10 minutes beforehand. Alternatively, use a griddle or frying pan.

Heat a dry frying pan, add the rice and toast until golden but not burnt. Grind the rice in a coffee-grinder or pound to a powder in a pestle and mortar and set aside. Reheat the frying pan and add the dried chillies. Toast until they are smoky, tossing regularly, then grind or pound to a powder. Mix with the rice in a small bowl and set aside – you should have about 2 teaspoons in total.

If using a griddle or frying pan, place over a high heat until very hot. Cook the steak over medium-hot coals on the barbecue or in the pan for 10–12 minutes until well marked on the outside and rare to medium-rare inside. Place in a non-metallic bowl and leave to rest for 10 minutes, then mix together the sesame oil and *ketjap manis* and brush all over the fillet. Cover with clingfilm and leave to marinate in a cool place for 2 hours, turning from time to time.

Place the cucumber, shallots, cherry tomatoes, chilli, herbs and spring onions in a large bowl and gently toss together to combine. Cover with clingfilm and chill until needed. Dissolve the sugar in the lime juice and fish sauce in a screw-top jar. Set aside until needed.

To serve, thinly slice the beef and return it to the bowl of marinade. Combine the cucumber mixture with the fish sauce dressing and ground chilli rice. Divide the salad leaves between plates and pile the beef mixture on top to serve.

Italian Bean Salad
with Griddled Red Onion

Serves 4 | VEGETARIAN

2 red onions, peeled and cut into wedges, root left intact

120ml (4fl oz) extra-virgin olive oil

juice of ½ lemon

pinch of caster sugar

2 x 400g cans of cannellini beans, drained and rinsed

15g (½oz) fresh flat-leaf parsley, stalks removed and roughly chopped

salt and freshly ground black pepper

This salad makes excellent picnic food, a fairly instant lunch or a great addition to an antipasti platter. It is best served at room temperature.

Preheat a griddle pan or heavy-based frying pan over a high heat. Toss the onion wedges in a bowl with 2 tablespoons of the oil and season generously with salt and pepper. Add to the griddle pan and cook for 6–8 minutes, turning occasionally, until cooked through and lightly charred.

Meanwhile, prepare the dressing. Place the remaining olive oil in a screw-top jar along with the lemon juice and sugar, and season with salt and pepper. Screw the lid on tightly, shake until well combined, then pour into a serving dish. When the onions are cooked through, add them to the dish, turn gently to coat in the dressing, then fold in the beans and parsley. Add seasoning to taste and serve at once.

Piedmont Roasted Peppers
with Feta Cheese

Serves 4 | VEGETARIAN

These peppers are roasted with their stalks still attached. Although the stalks are not edible, they do look attractive and help the peppers keep their shape while cooking. This makes a fantastic starter or lovely side dish for a barbecue. For a change, you could omit the feta cheese and sprinkle each pepper half with thinly sliced garlic before roasting.

4 large red peppers

6 tbsp extra-virgin olive oil

4 ripe tomatoes

225g (8oz) feta cheese, crumbled

Maldon sea salt and freshly ground black pepper

fresh basil leaves, to garnish

Preheat the oven to 180°C (350°F), gas mark 4. Cut the peppers in half and remove the seeds and membranes but leave the stalks intact. Lightly oil a roasting tin and add the pepper halves.

Place the tomatoes in a bowl and pour boiling water over them. This will make the skins easier to remove. Leave for 1 minute, then drain and transfer to a bowl of iced water. Once the tomatoes are cool enough to handle, peel off the skins using a knife or your fingers, then cut into quarters and place two quarters into each pepper half.

Sprinkle salt and pepper over the filled pepper halves and splash the remaining olive oil on top. Roast for 50–60 minutes until the peppers are completely tender and lightly charred around the edges.

Transfer the peppers to plates and spoon over all of the cooking juices from the tin. Scatter over the feta cheese and garnish with the basil leaves. Serve warm or at room temperature.

Chargrilled Vegetable Layered Sandwich

with Tapenade

Serves 4–6

225ml (8fl oz) olive oil

2 garlic cloves, peeled and crushed

4 dried small red chillies

1 tbsp chopped fresh flat-leaf parsley

3 small courgettes, sliced lengthways

2 red peppers, cut into quarters and seeds removed

2 yellow peppers, cut into quarters and seeds removed

2 red onions, peeled and sliced into thick rounds

1 aubergine, cut into 1cm (½in) rounds

1 rustic round loaf, measuring about 25cm (10in) across

4 tbsp tapenade (see page 18 or shop-bought)

small bunch of fresh basil, leaves finely torn

2 x 100g (4oz) balls of mozzarella, very thinly sliced

40g (1½oz) wild rocket

salt and freshly ground black pepper

Begin preparations for this layered up loaf the day before you want to eat it. You can experiment with flavours – try red or green pesto for a vegetarian alternative to the tapenade, or add a layer of spinach or watercress. Different cheeses, smoked salmon or even fresh white crabmeat would all taste great with the chargrilled vegetables.

Place the olive oil in a shallow, non-metallic dish, stir in the garlic, chillies and parsley and add salt and pepper. Add the courgettes, peppers and onions, and leave to marinate at room temperature for 1 hour if time allows. Toss the aubergine in the marinade at the last minute so that it doesn't absorb too much of the oil.

If cooking on a barbecue, arrange the vegetables on the grill rack over medium–hot coals and cook for 6–8 minutes until completely softened and richly coloured, turning regularly and lightly basting with any remaining marinade. Alternatively, cook in batches on a heated griddle pan, following instructions as above.

Meanwhile, cut a 1cm (½in) slice off the top of the loaf. Hollow out the bread with your fingers to leave a case with 'walls' about 1cm (½in) thick. Brush the inside of the loaf with a little of the leftover marinade and spread lightly with two-thirds of the tapenade.

Once the vegetables are cooked, remove from the grill and layer up inside the loaf, sprinkling each layer with basil and seasoning. Begin with the aubergine, then the sliced mozzarella, the red peppers, yellow peppers, onions and courgettes. Spread over the remaining tapenade and cover with the rocket, pressing it down gently.

Replace the top of the bread and wrap the whole loaf in a sheet of greaseproof paper and then a large piece of clingfilm. Place the filled loaf in the fridge overnight between two wooden chopping boards and weigh down – lots of unopened cans will do the trick. To serve, allow the filled loaf to come back to room temperature, then unwrap and cut into thick wedges. Perfect for a picnic!

Shallot Tarte Tatin

550g (1lb 4oz) banana shallots

50g (2oz) unsalted butter

300ml (10fl oz) vegetable stock (see page 213)

225g (8oz) all-butter puff pastry, thawed if frozen

2 tbsp caster sugar

1 tbsp balsamic vinegar

½ tsp chopped fresh thyme

salt and freshly ground black pepper

lightly dressed green salad, to serve

This tart is delicious made with all-butter puff pastry. Most major supermarkets now sell this, and it tastes so much better than the regular variety that it's worth seeking out.

Soak the shallots in a bowl of boiling water for 5 minutes, then drain and peel. Trim off the roots. Melt 40g (1½oz) of the butter in a large frying or sauté pan set over a low heat. Gently fry the shallots for about 10 minutes, tossing occasionally, until golden. Add the stock and simmer for another 5–10 minutes, depending on the size of the shallots, until they are tender but still holding their shape. Remove with a slotted spoon, drain well and pat dry with kitchen paper. (If you wish, save the stock and use later for sauces or soup.) Leave to cool completely.

Preheat the oven to 190°C (375°F), gas mark 5. Roll out the pastry on a lightly floured board and cut out a 25cm (10in) circle, using a large plate as a template. Transfer to a baking sheet and chill for at least 30 minutes to allow the pastry to rest.

Melt the rest of the butter in a 23cm (9in) ovenproof, non-stick frying pan set over a medium heat. Add the shallots and toss until well coated and heated through. Sprinkle over the sugar and cook for a minute or two until caramelised, tossing constantly. Sprinkle over the vinegar and thyme, toss again, and remove from the heat.

Season the shallots generously with salt and pepper. Put the pastry circle on top, tucking the edges down the sides of the pan. Bake in the oven for about 30 minutes or until the pastry is well risen and golden brown. Leave for a few minutes before loosening the sides with a knife and inverting onto a flat plate. Serve warm or cold, cut into slices with some fresh green salad.

VARIATION

While the tart is still warm, scatter over 100g (4oz) of crumbled blue cheese, such as Stilton or Roquefort. If the cheese doesn't melt from the warmth of the tart, simply flash under the grill.

Pumpkin, Spinach and Chickpea Curry
with Flatbread

Serves 4 | VEGETARIAN

about 6 tbsp sunflower oil

1 onion, peeled and thinly sliced

2 garlic cloves, peeled and crushed

2.5cm (1in) piece of fresh root ginger, grated

1 green chilli, seeded and finely chopped

2 tbsp Madras (hot) curry powder

700ml (1¼ pints) vegetable stock (see page 213)

2 ripe vine tomatoes, peeled and chopped

350g (12oz) pumpkin flesh, cut into cubes

400g can of chickpeas, drained and rinsed

225g (8oz) tender young spinach

2 tbsp thick Greek yoghurt

salt and freshly ground black pepper

For the flatbread

4 tbsp thick Greek yoghurt

1 egg, lightly beaten

225g (8oz) self-raising flour, plus extra for dusting

1 green chilli, seeded and finely chopped

2 tbsp chopped fresh coriander, plus extra to garnish

sunflower oil, for greasing

about 25g (1oz) butter

Vegetarian dishes form a large part of the southern Indian diet, and this one is particularly tasty. The flatbreads can be made in minutes, so don't be tempted to prepare too far in advance or they will begin to harden. Alternatively, you can use shop-bought naan bread.

Heat 2 tablespoons of the oil in a large pan with a lid, then sauté the onion over a low heat for 5 minutes until soft and just starting to brown. Add the garlic, ginger and half the chilli and continue to cook for 1 minute, stirring constantly. Stir in the curry powder and cook for another minute, then add the stock and tomatoes and stir to combine. Bring to a simmer, season, and add the pumpkin. Cover and simmer for 15–20 minutes until the pumpkin is tender but still holding its shape.

To make the flatbreads, heat a large, non-stick griddle or frying pan. Mix the yoghurt in a measuring jug with enough warm water to make 120ml (4fl oz), then stir in the beaten egg. Sift the flour and half a teaspoon of salt into a bowl. Make a well in the centre, add the yoghurt mixture, chilli and coriander and quickly mix to a soft but not sticky dough, adding more warm water if necessary.

Turn out the dough onto a lightly floured work surface and knead for about 30 seconds until smooth. Divide into four portions, then use a rolling pin to roll each piece to an oval no more than 5mm (¼in) thick. Add a thin film of oil to the heated griddle pan and cook a piece of dough for 4–5 minutes on each side until cooked through and lightly golden. Remove from the pan, pat dry with kitchen paper, then wrap in a clean tea towel while you cook the rest.

Add the chickpeas and raw spinach to the pumpkin mixture and cook for a few minutes until heated through and the spinach has wilted. Stir in the yoghurt and gently warm through. Spread butter over the warm flatbreads. Divide the curry into warmed bowls set on serving plates and garnish with the coriander. Place a buttered flatbread to the side of each one and serve.

Roasted Stuffed Aubergines
with Goat's Cheese and Cherry Tomatoes

Serves 4 | VEGETARIAN

It's not without reason that in the Middle East aubergines are still regarded as the poor man's meat. They make an excellent vegetarian main course or light lunch, as they are so rich in nutrients. Prepare this recipe in advance and simply pop in the oven just before you are ready to serve.

2 large aubergines

3 tbsp olive oil

1 red pepper

1 shallot, peeled and finely chopped

small handful of fresh basil leaves, torn

225g (8oz) cherry tomatoes, halved

2 x 100g (4oz) individual goat's cheeses (with rind), thinly sliced

Maldon sea salt and freshly ground black pepper

lightly dressed green salad, to serve

Preheat the oven to 200°C (400°F), gas mark 6. Cut the aubergines in half lengthways and trim off the stalks. Brush the cut sides with a little of the oil and season with salt and pepper, then place in a roasting tin with the whole red pepper and bake for 30–35 minutes or until the flesh of the aubergine is tender and the skin of the red pepper is blackened and blistered.

Meanwhile, heat a tablespoon of the oil in a frying pan set over a medium heat and sauté the shallot for 2–3 minutes until softened but not browned. Set aside.

Remove the roasted vegetables from the oven (leaving the oven turned on), and once the red pepper is cool, peel away the skin and finely chop the flesh, discarding the seeds. Place in a bowl with the sautéed shallot. Scoop out the flesh from the aubergines, to within 1cm (½in) of the skin, and finely chop the removed flesh. Add to the red pepper and shallot, then add the basil and season generously with salt and pepper.

Pile the mixture back into the aubergine shells and arrange the cherry tomatoes and slices of goat's cheese on top. Drizzle over the remaining oil and return to the oven for 20–25 minutes until the cherry tomatoes are lightly charred and the goat's cheese is bubbling. Arrange on plates with the lightly dressed salad to serve.

Stir-fried Baby Pak Choi
with Mushrooms

Serves 4 | VEGETARIAN

2 tbsp sunflower oil

6 spring onions, trimmed and cut on the diagonal into 5cm (2in) pieces

2 garlic cloves, peeled and crushed

2.5cm (1in) piece of fresh root ginger, peeled and cut into fine julienne strips

2 lemongrass stalks, outer leaves removed and the core finely chopped

1 red chilli, seeded and very thinly sliced

100g (4oz) shiitake mushrooms, trimmed and sliced

400g (14oz) white baby pak choi (or green if preferred)

1 tbsp oyster sauce

1 tbsp dark soy sauce

2 tsp toasted sesame seeds

handful of fresh coriander leaves, to garnish

This very simple recipe is one of my favourite ways of preparing baby pak choi. You can use the white or green varieties, or you could use regular-sized pak choi cut crossways into 2.5cm (1in) wide strips. This recipe is excellent served with Tea-smoked Barbary duck (see page 45).

Heat the sunflower oil in a wok or deep, heavy-based frying pan. Add the spring onions, garlic, ginger, lemongrass and chilli and stir-fry for 1 minute.

Add the shiitake mushrooms to the pan and continue to stir-fry for 2–3 minutes until tender. Tip in the pak choy and stir-fry for a further minute, then sprinkle over a tablespoon of water, reduce the heat and stir-fry for another 2–3 minutes or until wilted.

Add the oyster sauce and soy sauce and toss the vegetables together briefly until coated, then scatter over the sesame seeds and toss to combine. Tip into a warmed serving bowl, scatter over the coriander leaves and serve immediately.

Oven-baked Tomatoes
with Ratatouille and a Basil Crust

Serves 4 | VEGETARIAN

Serve these tasty stuffed tomatoes on their own or, for a more substantial meal, with grilled goat's cheese. Look in your local supermarket for tomatoes that have been grown specifically for flavour. (What did they used to be grown for? It makes you wonder. . .)

Preheat the oven to 180°C (350°F), gas mark 4. Heat a heavy-based frying pan. Add a tablespoon of olive oil and sauté the onion and garlic for a couple of minutes until softened but not browned, stirring occasionally. Stir in the courgette, aubergine and red pepper and continue to sauté for 5 minutes until the vegetables begin to soften. Stir in the tomato purée, balsamic vinegar, sugar and oregano and gently cook for 5 minutes, stirring occasionally. Season with salt and pepper and keep warm.

Trim a 1cm (¼in) slice off the top of each tomato and discard, then carefully scoop out the pulp with a teaspoon. (Reserve the pulp for another recipe, such as chilli jam (see page 107) or red pepper and tomato sauce (see page 150).) Carefully spoon the ratatouille mixture into the tomato shells.

Put the breadcrumbs in a mini blender along with the basil and the remaining tablespoon of olive oil, then blitz until green in colour. Season with salt and pepper and sprinkle the crumbs on top of the stuffed tomatoes. Arrange in a roasting tin lined with non-stick parchment paper and bake for 10–15 minutes until the tomatoes are heated through and the basil crumbs are crisp. Be careful not to overcook or the tomatoes will lose their shape. Using a fish slice, transfer two stuffed vine tomatoes onto each warmed plate. These are excellent served alongside the Parma-wrapped Pork Fillet Stuffed with Pesto (see page 72).

2 tbsp olive oil

1 small onion, peeled and diced

1 garlic clove, peeled and crushed

1 small courgette, finely diced

1 small aubergine, finely diced

1 red pepper, halved, seeded and finely diced

1 tsp tomato purée

1 tsp balsamic vinegar

1 tsp caster sugar

1 tsp chopped fresh oregano

8 large vine tomatoes

2 tbsp fresh white breadcrumbs

1 tbsp torn fresh basil

Maldon sea salt and freshly ground black pepper

Griddled Asparagus
with Roasted Red Peppers and Parmesan

Serves 6 | VEGETARIAN

2 bunches of asparagus (about 24 spears in total)

4 tbsp extra-virgin olive oil

6 fresh basil leaves, torn

3 fresh thyme sprigs

1 tbsp chopped fresh flat-leaf parsley

3 large red peppers

4 garlic cloves, unpeeled

300ml (10fl oz) balsamic vinegar

50g (2oz) toasted pine nuts

75g (3oz) Parmesan shavings, to garnish

25g (1oz) wild rocket, to garnish

Maldon sea salt and freshly ground black pepper

Of course, this is best eaten during the asparagus season, which runs for approximately eight weeks in May and June. This is when asparagus has a full, sweet flavour and fine texture. Baby leeks make a good winter alternative.

To prepare the asparagus spears, trim about 5cm (2in) of the woody ends from each spear. Bring a large saucepan of salted water to the boil and blanch the asparagus tips for 2 minutes, then drain and quickly refresh in a bowl of iced water. Drain again and dry thoroughly, then place in a non-metallic dish.

Add 2 tablespoons of the olive oil and the basil, thyme and parsley to the asparagus spears, turning to coat them evenly. Cover with clingfilm and leave to marinate for 1 hour (or overnight in the fridge).

Preheat the oven to 200ºC (400ºF), gas mark 6. Place the red peppers in a roasting tin with the garlic and drizzle over the remaining olive oil. Roast for 30–40 minutes until the skins are well charred and the peppers are completely tender.

Remove the roasted peppers from the oven and carefully place them in a plastic food bag. Tie securely and leave to cool completely – the steam will make it easier to remove the skins. Once the peppers are cool, remove from the bag and peel off the skins. Cut each pepper in half, then discard the cores and seeds and set aside until needed.

Peel the garlic cloves, then mash the flesh to a paste and stir into the marinating asparagus mixture.

To make a balsamic syrup, place the balsamic vinegar in a heavy-based saucepan and bring to the boil. Simmer for 15–20 minutes, stirring occasionally, until it reaches a syrup-like consistency. Leave to cool and then transfer to a plastic squeezy bottle. This will keep happily in the fridge for up to three months.

When ready to serve, heat a griddle pan or heavy-based frying pan until very hot. Add the roasted peppers to the asparagus ○

mixture, tossing to coat in the marinade, then season lightly with salt and pepper. Carefully arrange the asparagus and peppers on the griddle pan and cook for 3 minutes, turning once until lightly charred and heated through. You may have to do this in batches, depending on the size of your griddle or frying pan.

To serve, arrange one pepper half and four asparagus spears on each warmed plate. Scatter over the toasted pine nuts and drizzle around some of the balsamic syrup. Garnish with the Parmesan shavings and wild rocket.

Beetroot Carpaccio
with Creamed Goat's Cheese

Serves 4 | VEGETARIAN

2 large raw beetroots

450ml (15fl oz) red wine

100ml (3½fl oz) ruby red port

2 tbsp crème de cassis (optional)

2 tsp caster sugar

225g (8oz) soft goat's cheese, any rind removed

3 tbsp basil oil (see page 219)

1 tsp snipped fresh chives

4 tsp balsamic syrup (see page 130 or shop-bought)

1 punnet of salad cress

1 small Granny Smith apple

4 tsp toasted pine nuts

Maldon sea salt and freshly ground black pepper

This is so simple to make and the vivid colours and intense flavours make it an impressive dish to serve to guests. The marinated beetroot will keep for up to two weeks in the fridge.

It is best to wear a pair of rubber gloves when preparing the beetroot, to avoid staining your hands. Trim the tops off the beetroots and then peel them with a knife. Using a mandolin or very sharp knife, carefully slice each beetroot as thinly as possible. You'll need 24 even-sized round slices in total.

Place the red wine in a large pan along with the port, crème de cassis, if using, and the sugar. Bring to the boil, then add the thinly sliced beetroot and cook for 8–10 minutes or until just cooked through. Leave to cool in the cooking syrup, then place in the fridge overnight if time allows. Once marinated, drain the beetroot well and reserve the syrup to use again for poaching pears or plums or for marinating more beetroot.

Place the goat's cheese in a food processor with 2 tablespoons of the basil oil and blend until soft. Stir in the chives and add salt and pepper to taste. Spoon into a piping bag fitted with a 2.5cm (1in) plain nozzle and chill for 10 minutes to help the mixture to firm up.

Immediately before serving, core the apple and shred into very fine strips. Drizzle each plate with a little balsamic syrup and arrange three slices of beetroot next to each other on top. Pipe the creamed goat's cheese onto the centre of each portion of beetroot and then carefully place another slice on top of each. Cut the salad cress with scissors and scatter on top with the apple strips and pine nuts, then drizzle over the remaining basil oil.

BENVINGUT A.

BIENVENIDO A.

WELCOME TO.

BIENVENU A.

WILLKOMMEN IN.

SOLLER

Baked Mediterranean Vegetables
with Tomato, Cooleeney Cheese and Parmesan

Serves 4 | VEGETARIAN

This dish uses Cooleeney cheese, which is soft and mould-ripened with a beautiful creamy texture and a distinctive aftertaste. It is produced on the Maher farm in the heart of Tipperary, Southern Ireland, where the pastures are rich and lush. However, if you have difficulty getting hold of it, try using a well-flavoured Camembert or goat's cheese instead.

Preheat the oven to 180ºC (350ºF), gas mark 4. Heat 2 tablespoons of the olive oil in a large frying pan. Add the red onion and sauté for a couple of minutes until lightly browned. Add the red pepper, garlic and aubergine, season with salt and pepper and cook over a low heat for 12–15 minutes until softened, stirring occasionally.

When cooked, scatter the sautéed vegetables over the bottom of an ovenproof dish. Cut the tomatoes and courgettes into thick rounds and arrange in overlapping rows on top of the sautéed vegetables. Cover with the slices of cheese and sprinkle over the thyme and basil. Season generously with salt and pepper, then drizzle over the remaining olive oil and bake for 30 minutes until all the vegetables are just cooked through and the cheese is bubbling.

Remove the dish from the oven and sprinkle over the breadcrumbs and Parmesan, then return to oven for 10 minutes to form a lightly golden crust. Serve with bowls of the green salad and crusty bread.

5 tbsp extra-virgin olive oil

1 red onion, peeled and cut into chunks

1 large red pepper, halved, seeded and cut into chunks

1 garlic clove, peeled and crushed

1 large aubergine, cut into cubes

450g (1lb) vine tomatoes

450g (1lb) small courgettes

175g (6oz) Cooleeney or Camembert cheese, sliced

1 tsp chopped fresh thyme

1 tbsp torn fresh basil leaves

2 tbsp fresh white breadcrumbs

2 tbsp freshly grated Parmesan cheese

salt and freshly ground black pepper

lightly dressed green salad and crusty bread, to serve

Goat's Cheese Pâté
with Apricot Relish

Serves 4–6

The creamy saltiness of goat's cheese goes perfectly with this sweet and sour apricot relish. When in season, you could use two firm, ripe apricots or even peaches instead of the dried apricots. Vegetarian gelatine is available from health food shops; it's made from seaweed and would work equally well in this recipe – just follow the packet instructions.

If using gelatine leaves, soften in a bowl of cold water for 10 minutes. Place the cream in a small saucepan and bring to a simmer. Drain and gently squeeze dry the soaked gelatine leaves, then whisk into the cream mixture for 1 minute until the gelatine has fully dissolved. If using powdered gelatine, simply whisk into the cream in a thin steady stream and continue to whisk for 1 minute until dissolved. Stir in the lemon juice.

Meanwhile, break up the goat's cheese into a bowl and add the pepper and herbs. Stir in the cream and gelatine mixture until well combined. Lay out a sheet of foil and cover with a layer of clingfilm, then spread the goat's cheese mixture onto the middle and roll up into a log. Twist the ends of the foil and clingfilm to secure. Chill for at least 4 hours or overnight.

To make the apricot relish, heat the oil in a large, heavy-based frying pan set over a low heat and gently sauté the onions for 10 minutes until well softened but not browned. Add the apricots, wine, vinegar, honey and salt and bring to the boil, stirring constantly. Reduce the heat and simmer for about 30 minutes until the liquid has almost totally reduced. Transfer to a bowl and leave to cool completely.

To serve, remove the foil and clingfilm wrapper from the pâté and cut into slices. Arrange three slices in the centre of each plate and surround with spoonfuls of the apricot relish. Serve at once with a separate basket of warm crusty bread.

2 gelatine leaves or 1 sachet powdered gelatine

150ml (5fl oz) double cream

juice of ½ lemon

450g (1lb) soft goat's cheese

1 tbsp snipped fresh chives

1 tbsp chopped fresh flat-leaf parsley

1 tbsp torn fresh basil leaves

1 tsp coarsely ground black pepper

warm crusty bread, to serve

For the apricot relish

1 tbsp olive oil

2 onions, peeled and finely chopped

175g (6oz) ready-to-eat dried apricots (or 2 fresh ripe apricots when in season), finely chopped

350ml (12fl oz) white wine

1 tbsp white wine vinegar

2 tbsp clear honey

1 tsp salt

Quick Quesadillas
with Chilli Salsa and Soured Cream

Serves 4 | VEGETARIAN

8 soft flour tortillas

2 tbsp olive oil, plus extra for brushing

225g (8oz) Cheddar cheese, grated

1 mild red chilli, seeded and finely chopped

4 spring onions, trimmed and finely chopped

salt and freshly ground black pepper

about 120ml (4fl oz) soured cream, to garnish

For the chilli salsa

225g (8oz) ripe vine tomatoes, seeded and diced

1 small red onion, peeled and diced

2 tbsp chopped fresh coriander, plus extra leaves to garnish

1 mild red chilli, seeded and finely chopped

juice of ½ lime

2 tbsp extra-virgin olive oil

salt and freshly ground black pepper

These quesadillas make a perfect lunch or mid-morning snack for all the family. They can be prepared up to 1 hour in advance, then covered with clingfilm and kept at room temperature. Simply flash them in the oven when you're ready to eat.

To make the chilli salsa, place the tomatoes in a non-metallic bowl with the red onion, chopped coriander, chilli, lime juice and olive oil, stirring until well combined. Season with salt and pepper, cover with clingfilm and leave at room temperature to allow the flavours to develop.

Preheat the oven to 200ºC (400ºF), gas mark 6 and heat a griddle pan or heavy-based frying pan over a medium heat until very hot. Brush one side of each tortilla with a little of the olive oil. Place one tortilla in the pan, oiled-side down, and cook for 1 minute until nicely marked, pressing down occasionally with a spatula. Repeat with the remaining tortillas. You do not need to cook the other side.

Arrange half the tortillas on non-stick baking trays, marked-side down. Sprinkle cheese over each one, then scatter with the chilli and spring onions and season with salt and pepper. Cover with the remaining tortillas, marked-side up, and bake for about 5 minutes or until heated through and the cheese has melted. Allow to cool slightly until easy to handle.

Cut each quesadilla into eight wedges with a serrated knife, pizza cutter or kitchen scissors. Garnish each wedge with a small spoonful of soured cream and a coriander leaf. Arrange on warmed plates or one large platter to serve, with a separate bowl of the chilli salsa to hand around.

Pizza Brie Tart

Serves 4 | VEGETARIAN

This versatile tart has all the familiar pizza flavours but with a crisp puff pastry base. If you use all-butter puff pastry, which is now widely available, the flavour is so much better. If you don't fancy using Brie, try slices of mozzarella or goat's cheese instead.

Roll out the pastry on a lightly floured board to a thickness of 5mm (¼in), then chill in the fridge for at least 30 minutes. Meanwhile, preheat the oven to 190°C (375°F), gas mark 5.

Cut four 20cm (8in) circles from the pastry, using a plate as a template, and prick the whole surface evenly with a fork. Place on non-stick baking trays and bake for 10–15 minutes until puffed up and lightly golden.

While the pastry is baking, heat the butter and the olive oil in a large frying pan and sauté the courgettes, red pepper, onion and mushrooms for a few minutes until just softened but not fully cooked. Season with salt and pepper and leave to cool a little.

Remove the pastry from the oven and lower the oven temperature to 180°C (350°F), gas mark 4. Brush the pastry with a little of the egg yolk to stop the pastry absorbing excess liquid from the vegetables, then toss the rest with the vegetables and Parmesan.

Spread the tossed vegetables evenly over the pastry bases and scatter the slices of Brie cheese on top. Return to the oven for about 10 minutes until the pizzas are puffed and golden and the vegetables are cooked. Cut into wedges, garnish with the basil leaves and serve on hot plates.

550g (1¼lb) ready-made puff pastry, thawed if frozen

a little plain flour, for dusting

25g (1oz) unsalted butter

1 tbsp olive oil

2 small courgettes, finely sliced

1 large red pepper, seeded and sliced

1 large red onion, peeled and finely sliced

225g (8oz) button mushrooms, sliced

2 large egg yolks, lightly beaten

50g (2oz) Parmesan cheese, freshly grated

175g (6oz) Brie cheese (ripe but firm), cut into thin slices

salt and freshly ground black pepper

fresh basil leaves, to garnish

Warm Crab and Spinach Tart

Serves 6

You can make the pastry case for this tart up to 24 hours in advance, but if you're short on time you could always use shop-bought pastry or even a ready-made pastry case instead. When I go to the trouble of making pastry, normally I make double the quantity and then freeze the leftovers for up to a month.

Preheat the oven to 200°C (400°F), gas mark 6. To make the pastry, place the flour, butter and chilli flakes in a food processor. Add half a teaspoon of salt and whiz briefly until the mixture forms fine crumbs. Pour in the water through the feeder tube and pulse again so that the pastry comes together. Knead gently on a lightly floured surface for a few seconds to make a smooth dough. Wrap in clingfim and chill for at least 10 minutes before rolling (or up to an hour if time allows).

Roll out the pastry on a lightly floured surface and line a loose-bottomed 21cm (8½in) fluted flan tin that is about 4cm (1½in) deep. Use a rolling pin to lift the pastry into the tin, pressing well into the sides and letting the pastry overhang a little as this prevents shrinkage. Chill for another 10 minutes.

Prick the pastry base with a fork, then line with a circle of oiled foil or non-stick baking paper (crumple it up to make it easier to handle). Fill with baking beans or dried pulses and bake for 10 minutes until the pastry case looks 'set', but not browned. Carefully remove the foil or paper and lower the temperature to 160°C (325°F), gas mark 3, then brush with the egg wash to form a seal. Return to the oven for another 5 minutes or until the base is firm to the touch and the sides are lightly browned.

Heat the butter in a saucepan and tip in the spinach. Sauté for a minute or two until wilted, then season to taste. Leave the spinach until cool enough to handle, then squeeze dry and finely chop.

In a bowl, beat together the cream, milk, chilli sauce, eggs and egg yolks until well combined. Stir in the parsley and season to taste. Scatter the finely chopped spinach and crabmeat over the bottom of the pastry case and sprinkle the Parmesan on top, ◗

knob of butter

350g (12oz) spinach leaves, tough stalks removed

150ml (5fl oz) double cream

150ml (5fl oz) milk

2 tbsp sweet chilli sauce

2 eggs

2 egg yolks

1 tbsp chopped fresh flat-leaf parsley

200g (7oz) white crabmeat

100g (4oz) Parmesan cheese, freshly grated

salt and freshly ground black pepper

For the pastry

225g (8oz) plain flour, plus extra for dusting

100g (4oz) butter, diced and chilled

pinch of dried chilli flakes

3 tbsp ice-cold water

egg wash (1 full egg with a little milk), for brushing

lightly dressed green salad, to serve

then pour in the cream mixture and bake for about 25 minutes until the filling is just set but still slightly wobbly in the middle. Leave to rest for 5 minutes in the tin, then remove and trim down the excess pastry. To serve, while still warm carefully cut the crab and spinach tart into slices. Arrange on plates with the salad.

VARIATION

Onion tart with mozzarella and sun-blushed dried tomatoes

Heat a tablespoon of olive oil in a heavy-based frying pan with a good knob of butter. Sweat 3 thinly sliced Spanish onions for about 30 minutes until well reduced and nicely caramelised, stirring regularly to prevent them sticking. Season to taste and stir in half a teaspoon of chopped fresh thyme. Leave to cool completely, then spread over the bottom of the pastry case. Scatter over 225g (8oz) of cubed mozzarella cheese and 100g (4oz) chopped sun-blushed tomatoes. Replace the parsley with torn fresh basil leaves and finish as described above.

Pancetta Frittata

Serves 4

Originating from Sicily, a frittata is excellent for a picnic or as a delicious light lunch or supper. The sweetness of the onions in this version perfectly complements the smokiness of the bacon. It's good served hot or cold.

2 tbsp olive oil

25g (1oz) unsalted butter

3 large onions, peeled and thinly sliced

175g (6oz) piece of pancetta, cut into small lardons

1 tsp fresh thyme leaves

3 garlic cloves, peeled and crushed

8 large eggs, beaten

50g (2oz) Parmesan cheese, freshly grated

1 tsp finely chopped fresh sage

salt and freshly ground black pepper

lightly dressed green salad, to serve

Heat 1 tablespoon of the oil with the butter in a large sauté or frying pan. Add the onions and start to cook over a fairly high heat, stirring constantly until softened but not browned, then reduce the heat to medium and continue to cook, stirring frequently so they do not stick or brown. The onions will need about 30 minutes in total to caramelise.

Stir the pancetta into the onion mixture with the thyme and garlic 5 minutes before the end of cooking time and continue to cook until the pancetta has begun is sizzle and crisp up. Tip into a large bowl and leave to cool for at least 5 minutes. Season generously.

Preheat the oven to 180°C (350°F), gas mark 4. Add the eggs, Parmesan and sage to the onions and stir well to combine. Heat the remaining oil in a heavy-based ovenproof frying pan, 23cm (9in) in diameter and deep enough to take the mixture (approximately 1.2 litres (2 pints)). Swirl to coat the sides of the pan evenly, then pour in the egg mixture and cook for 6–8 minutes over a low heat to set the bottom and sides.

Transfer the pan to the oven and cook, uncovered, for about 20 minutes until just set, puffed up and lightly golden. Loosen the sides with a palette knife and cut the frittata into wedges and serve warm or cold, straight from the pan. Have a separate bowl of the salad on the table and allow guests to help themselves.

VARIATION

Greek-style omelette

Add two peeled, seeded and finely chopped tomatoes to the onion mixture instead of the pancetta and use crumbled feta cheese instead of the Parmesan. Cook as described above.

pulses, grains and pasta

Smoked Salmon and Saffron Orzo

2 large pinches of saffron threads

350g (12oz) orzo pasta

225ml (8fl oz) double cream

finely grated rind of 1 lemon

1 tbsp torn fresh basil leaves

1 tbsp snipped fresh chives

350g (12oz) smoked salmon slices, diced

salt and freshly ground black pepper

Orzo is a rice-shaped pasta, each grain slightly smaller than a pine nut, made from hard wheat semolina. In Italy it is frequently used in soups. In the restaurant we often serve this dish topped with a piece of seared salmon or cod.

Bring a large saucepan of salted water to the boil and add the saffron. Tip in the orzo pasta, stir once, then cook for 12–15 minutes until just al dente or according to packet instructions. Drain the pasta well under cold running water.

Place the cream in a large, clean saucepan with the lemon rind. Bring to the boil, then reduce the heat and simmer for 2 minutes. Add the cooked orzo and simmer for another 5 minutes, stirring occasionally. Season with salt and pepper and stir in the herbs and diced salmon. Allow to warm through, then divide between four warmed bowls.

Tabbouleh Salad

This is a classic Middle Eastern salad made with cracked wheat, also known as bulgar or burghul wheat. You'll find it in health food shops or alongside the dried pulses and beans in the supermarket. I love this salad as it is so colourful and goes well with all types of barbecued food.

Place the bulgar wheat in a bowl and pour over enough cold water to cover it. Set aside for 3 minutes, then tip into a sieve and rinse well under cold running water. Drain well and tip back into the bowl.

Meanwhile, make the dressing for the tabbouleh. Place the lemon zest and juice in a screw-top jar along with the garlic, cinnamon and allspice. Season with salt and pepper, screw the lid on tightly and shake until the salt has dissolved. Add the olive oil, replace the lid and shake again until well combined.

Add the tomatoes to the drained bulgar wheat, along with the parsley, mint and spring onions. Stir until well combined, then pour in the dressing and toss until all the ingredients are evenly coated. Season with salt and pepper and set aside at room temperature for 30 minutes to allow the flavours to develop. Give the tabbouleh salad a good stir before serving.

200g (7oz) bulgar wheat

zest and juice of 1 lemon

2 garlic cloves, peeled and crushed

good pinch of ground cinnamon

good pinch of ground allspice

6 tbsp extra-virgin olive oil

4 ripe tomatoes, halved, seeded and diced

25g (1oz) roughly chopped fresh flat-leaf parsley

good handful of fresh mint leaves, roughly chopped

bunch of spring onions, trimmed and finely chopped

salt and freshly ground black pepper

Porcini and Artichoke Pasta
with Thyme and Lemon

Serves 4 | VEGETARIAN

25g (1oz) dried porcini mushrooms

2 tbsp olive oil

1 onion, peeled and diced

2 garlic cloves, peeled and crushed

1 tsp chopped fresh thyme

150ml (5fl oz) dry white wine

finely grated rind and juice of 1 lemon

450g (1lb) linguine pasta

150ml (5fl oz) double cream

300g jar of artichoke hearts in oil (or 400g can of artichoke hearts in brine), drained and cut in half

50g (2oz) Parmesan cheese, freshly grated, plus extra to garnish

50g (2oz) wild rocket

1 tbsp chopped fresh flat-leaf parsley

salt and freshly ground black pepper

Although porcini mushrooms are expensive, just a small amount added to a recipe will make an enormous difference to the flavour. Their savoury taste is intensely concentrated in this creamy pasta dish.

Place the porcini mushrooms in a small bowl and pour over enough boiling water to cover. Leave to stand for 20 minutes to rehydrate.

Heat the olive oil in a heavy-based frying pan. Tip in the onion and garlic and sauté for about 3 minutes until softened but not browned. Stir in the thyme, then pour in the wine and add the lemon juice and cook for 5 minutes until slightly reduced, stirring occasionally.

Drain the porcini mushrooms, reserving the liquid, and finely chop. Add to the wine mixture with the reserved soaking liquid and simmer for about 5 minutes or until reduced by half.

Meanwhile, cook the linguine pasta in a large saucepan of boiling salted water for 10–12 minutes until al dente or according to packet instructions.

Stir the cream into the reduced porcini mixture, then fold in the artichoke hearts and Parmesan. Simmer very gently for about 5 minutes until slightly thickened and heated through. Stir in rocket, parsley and lemon rind and cook for another 1–2 minutes until the rocket is just wilted. Season to taste.

Drain the pasta and shake well to remove any excess water, then return to the pan and stir in the porcini and artichoke sauce. Divide between warmed pasta bowls. Scatter over a little extra Parmesan to garnish. Serve at once.

Puy Lentil, Red Onion and
Sun-dried Tomato Salad

Serves 4 | VEGETARIAN

**Puy lentils are a greeny, slate-grey colour and definitely have
the best flavour of all types of lentils. If your supermarket
doesn't have any, you'll find them in a health food shop.
Or, if you're in a hurry, used canned puy lentils, which require
no cooking. I like to make this salad a few hours before
I need it, giving the flavours time to soak into the lentils.**

Place the lentils in a large saucepan with the bay leaf, vinegar, 1
garlic clove and the sugar. Season to taste and cover with 1.2 litres
(2 pints) of cold water. Bring to the boil, then reduce the heat and
simmer for 25 minutes or until the lentils are just tender but still
holding their shape.

Drain the lentils well, discarding the bay leaf and whole garlic
clove. Tip into a bowl and leave to cool completely.

Finely chop the remaining garlic clove and stir it into the lentils
with the red onion, sun-dried tomatoes, parsley, balsamic vinegar
and olive oil. Season to taste and stir well to combine, then
carefully fold in the goat's cheese or feta. Cover with clingfilm and
set aside at room temperature for 30 minutes to allow the
flavours to develop. To serve, divide between four plates and eat
with some crusty bread, if liked.

225g (8oz) Puy lentils,
washed

1 bay leaf

1 tsp red wine vinegar

2 garlic cloves, peeled

pinch of caster sugar

1 large red onion, peeled and
finely chopped

50g (2oz) sun-dried tomatoes
in oil, drained and chopped

4 tbsp coarsely chopped
fresh flat-leaf parsley

1 tbsp balsamic vinegar

4 tbsp extra-virgin olive oil

100g (4oz) goat's cheese or
feta cheese, crumbled

salt and freshly ground black
pepper

crusty bread, to serve
(optional)

Swiss Chard and Ricotta Ravioli
with Parmesan Shavings and Toasted Pine Nuts

Serves 4 | VEGETARIAN

1 tbsp olive oil

1 small red onion, peeled and finely diced

2 garlic cloves, peeled and finely chopped

4 Swiss or ruby chard leaves, tough stalks removed (if unavailable, use 100g (4oz) tender young spinach leaves)

200g (7oz) ricotta cheese

1 tbsp torn fresh basil leaves

24 wonton wrappers, thawed if frozen

1-2 tbsp plain flour, for dusting

egg wash (1 full egg with 1 tbsp milk), for brushing

extra-virgin olive oil, for drizzling

25g (1oz) wild rocket

4 tbsp toasted pine nuts

25g (1oz) Parmesan, pared into shavings

salt and freshly ground black pepper

This dish will look as if you have gone to the trouble of making your own pasta. Instead, the secret is to use wonton wrappers, which can be found in Oriental supermarkets. However, the ravioli do need to be made fresh and don't benefit from hanging around.

Heat the olive oil in a frying pan and sauté the onion and garlic for about for 5 minutes until softened but not browned. Remove and set aside. Add the chard and cook for 2–3 minutes until just wilted, stirring regularly. Remove from the heat, drain and leave to cool completely.

Squeeze out any excess moisture from the chard mixture, then finely chop. Place in a bowl with the reserved onions and stir in the ricotta and basil. Season to taste and mix well to combine.

Place 12 wonton wrappers on a lightly floured work surface and spoon a heaped teaspoon of the chard mixture into the centre of each one. Brush around the edges with a little egg wash, then carefully cover with the remaining wonton wrappers, pressing gently to shape into ravioli. You can use a small fluted cutter to shape each ravioli, if you wish, discarding the leftover scraps of wonton pastry.

To cook the ravioli, bring a large saucepan of salted water to the boil. Add the ravioli and simmer for about 2 minutes until just cooked through and floating at the top of the pan. Drain well and arrange on warmed plates. Drizzle over the extra-virgin olive oil and scatter over the wild rocket, then sprinkle the toasted pine nuts and Parmesan shavings on top.

Singapore Noodles

Serves 4

You can buy all the ingredients for this dish from larger supermarkets, but for an extra-special dish it's worth taking a trip to an Oriental supermarket. There you will find Chinese dried mushrooms and shrimps, not to mention a fantastic range of rice noodles to choose from. The finished result will taste far better than any Chinese takeaway!

Place the dried mushrooms and shrimps in a bowl and pour over enough boiling water to cover. Set aside for 30 minutes to soak. Drain the liquid, but reserve 2 tablespoons and place in a bowl with the soy sauce and sherry. Set aside until needed. Squeeze the excess moisture from the drained mushrooms and chop into fine shreds.

Place the noodles in a large bowl, cover them with boiling water and leave to soak for 15 minutes, then drain well in a colander.

Heat the oil in a large wok or frying pan until very hot and almost smoking. Add the onion, garlic, ginger, shredded mushrooms and drained Chinese shrimps. Sauté for 10–15 minutes, moving the ingredients around gently until completely softened and all of the flavours have combined.

Stir the curry powder and the salt into the onion mixture and cook for another minute, stirring constantly. Tip in the chicken or pork, prawns and spring onions, stirring quickly to combine. Add the drained noodles, then, using either a large fork or some chopsticks, toss the ingredients so that everything is well combined.

Sprinkle the reserved soy sauce mixture over the Singapore noodles, then give everything a good stir and divide immediately between warm plates to serve.

12 Chinese dried mushrooms

2 heaped tbsp Chinese dried shrimps

2 tbsp light soy sauce

2 tbsp dry sherry

225g (8oz) rice noodles

2 tbsp groundnut oil

1 large onion, peeled and finely chopped

2 garlic cloves, peeled and finely chopped

1 tbsp freshly grated root ginger

1 tbsp Madras (hot) curry powder

100g (4oz) cooked skinless chicken or pork fillet, finely shredded

100g (4oz) cooked peeled prawns, chopped

bunch of spring onions, trimmed and finely chopped

good pinch of salt

Lemon and Herb Couscous
with Roasted Spicy Root Vegetables

Serves 4 | VEGETARIAN

Couscous is a staple of the North African diet and can be used to accompany tagines or with great success in salads. It is made from semolina grains that have been rolled, dampened and coated with very fine wheat flour. This enlarges the individual grains and keeps them separate during cooking.

To make the roasted spicy root vegetables, preheat the oven to 180°C (350°F), gas mark 4. Place the oil in a large roasting tin and add the carrots and parsnips, tossing until well coated. Season generously. Roast for 30 minutes until almost tender.

Meanwhile, place the couscous in a large heatproof bowl. Bring the stock to a simmer, then pour over the couscous. Stir well to combine, then cover and set aside for 15 minutes.

Remove the root vegetables from the oven, then drizzle over the honey and soy sauce and sprinkle the red chilli on top, tossing to coat evenly. Return to the oven and roast for another 10 minutes or until the vegetables are completely tender and lightly charred. Sprinkle over the sesame seeds and parsley and toss gently until evenly coated.

To finish the couscous, heat a frying pan with the olive oil. Sauté the onion, garlic and lemon rind for 2–3 minutes until softened but not browned. Remove from the heat. Gently separate the couscous grains with a fork. Season to taste and place in a saucepan to re-heat, stirring continuously with a fork. Fold in the onion mixture with the herbs. To serve, divide the couscous between four warmed plates and arrange the roasted spicy root vegetables on top.

225g (8oz) couscous

450ml (15fl oz) vegetable stock (see page 213)

2 tbsp olive oil

1 small red onion, peeled and finely diced

1 garlic clove, peeled and finely chopped

finely grated rind of 1 lemon

1 tbsp chopped fresh mixed herbs (such as flat-leaf parsley, basil and coriander)

salt and freshly ground black pepper

For the spicy root vegetables

3 tbsp olive oil

500g (1lb 2oz) carrots, peeled, trimmed and halved lengthways

500g (1lb 2oz) large parsnips, peeled, trimmed, quartered and cored

3 tbsp clear honey

2 tbsp light soy sauce

1 mild red chilli, seeded and finely chopped

1 tsp toasted sesame seeds

2 tbsp chopped fresh flat-leaf parsley

salt and freshly ground black pepper

Mussel and Saffron Risotto
with Leek and Courgette

Serves 4

One of Italy's great simple dishes, risotto is perfect comfort food and always very popular in the restaurant. The trick of a good risotto is to add the stock little by little, letting the liquid almost disappear before adding the next ladleful. This recipe is ideal for a dinner party or for lunch.

Place the mussels in a large saucepan set over a high heat. Add the onion with half of the leek, then pour in the wine and vegetable stock. Bring to the boil, then reduce the heat and simmer for a minute or two until all of the mussels have opened. Remove from heat and pass the stock through a large sieve or colander into a bowl. Remove the mussels from their shells and reserve; discard any that have not opened.

Pour the stock into a clean saucepan and bring to a gentle simmer. Heat the olive oil in a large sauté or frying pan. Tip in the rice and stir for 1 minute until the grains are glossy. Add the remaining leek with the courgette, garlic and saffron, stirring to combine.

Pour a ladleful of the simmering stock into the rice mixture and allow to bubble away, stirring from time to time. Continue to add the stock a ladleful at a time, stirring frequently. Allow each stock addition to be almost completely absorbed before adding the next ladleful, until the rice is al dente – tender on the outside, but still with a slight bite in the centre of the grain. This should take about 20 minutes.

Remove the risotto from the heat and stir in the herbs and Parmesan, then cover with a lid and leave to rest for 5 minutes. Stir in cooked mussel meat and allow to heat through. Season to taste and divide between four warmed wide-rimmed bowls. Garnish with herbs to serve.

450g (1lb) fresh mussels, cleaned

1 onion, peeled and thinly sliced

1 leek, trimmed and diced

150ml (5fl oz) white wine

1.2 litres (2 pints) vegetable stock (see page 213)

1 tbsp olive oil

225g (8oz) arborio (risotto) rice

1 small courgette, diced

2 garlic cloves, peeled and crushed

2 large pinches of saffron strands, soaked in a little warm water

4 tbsp chopped fresh mixed herbs (such as chives and flat-leaf parsley), plus extra to garnish

1 tbsp freshly grated Parmesan cheese

salt and freshly ground black pepper

Crispy Wild Mushroom
Risotto Balls
with Leek and Smoked Bacon

Serves 6–8

This recipe turns a basic risotto into wonderfully crisp balls. It's a great way to use up any leftover risotto (see page 177), or you can make it from scratch. They are always a hit with children, although the flavours in this version are quite grown up.

Soak the dried cep or porcini mushrooms in a bowl with 300ml (10fl oz) hot water. Melt half the butter in a large sauté or frying pan with half the oil, add the leek and smoked bacon and cook over a gentle heat for 2–3 minutes until the leek is softened and the bacon is sizzling. Add the fresh mushrooms and continue to sauté for 2–3 minutes until tender. Season to taste, then tip into a bowl and set aside until ready to use.

Pour the stock into a large saucepan and bring to a gentle simmer. Wipe out the pan that the mushroom mixture was cooked in and return to the heat. Add the remaining butter and oil, then tip in the onion, thyme and bay leaf and cook for a few minutes until softened but not browned, stirring regularly.

Add the rice to the onion mixture and continue to cook for another minute, stirring thoroughly to ensure that all the grains are well coated. Drain the cep mushrooms, reserving the liquid, then add the liquid to the pan and allow to bubble down, stirring until it has been completely absorbed. Meanwhile, chop the cep mushrooms and add them too.

Begin to add the simmering stock a ladle at a time, stirring frequently. Allow each stock addition to be almost completely absorbed before adding the next. After approximately 20 minutes, add the reserved mushroom mixture with half the Parmesan, the mascarpone and parsley, and stir energetically to combine. Season to taste and leave to cool completely.

Place the flour on a flat plate and season with salt and pepper. Whisk the eggs and milk in a bowl and season to taste. Mix together the remaining Parmesan with the breadcrumbs in a shallow dish. Using a small ice cream scoop, make balls of the cold risotto then lightly dust them in the seasoned flour. Dip in ⟳

7–15g (¼–½oz) dried cep or porcini mushrooms

50g (2oz) unsalted butter

2 tbsp olive oil

1 leek, trimmed and finely chopped

50g (2oz) piece of rindless smoked bacon, finely diced

125g (5oz) mixed fresh mushrooms (such as shiitake, chestnut, chanterelle and oyster), chopped

about 1 litre (1¾ pints) vegetable stock (see page 213)

1 onion, peeled and finely chopped

1 tsp fresh thyme leaves

1 bay leaf

225g (8oz) arborio (risotto) rice

75g (3oz) Parmesan cheese, freshly grated

75g (3oz) mascarpone cheese

2 tbsp chopped fresh flat-leaf parsley

50g (2oz) plain flour

2 eggs

2 tbsp milk

100g (4oz) toasted dried breadcrumbs

4 tbsp olive oil

salt and freshly ground black pepper

dressed bitter salad leaves, such as radicchio or rocket, to serve the beaten egg and then quickly roll them in the Parmesan breadcrumbs until well coated. Arrange on a baking sheet lined with non-stick baking paper and chill for at least 1 hour or overnight to firm up.

Heat the olive oil in a large, heavy-based frying pan and sauté the first batch of risotto balls for 6–8 minutes until crisp and golden brown, moving them around in the pan to ensure they cook evenly. Alternatively, you could cook in a deep-fat fryer at 160°C (325°F), turning regularly for 3–4 minutes until golden brown. Drain well on kitchen paper and keep warm while you cook the remainder. Arrange several risotto balls on each plate with some salad leaves to serve.

Baked Macaroni Pie
with Dublin Bay Prawns (Langoustines)

Serves 4

I have also made this delicious pie using undyed smoked haddock or cod with very successful results. If you do this, first poach the fish in a little water or milk, before breaking it into large flakes and discarding any skin and bones.

Preheat the oven to 220°C (425°F), gas mark 7. Carefully remove the cherry tomatoes from their vines and place in an ovenproof dish. Sprinkle with half the garlic and drizzle over the olive oil. Season with salt and pepper. Roast for 15 minutes until the tomatoes have softened slightly and skins have started to split, turning once or twice to ensure even cooking. Leave the oven on.

Meanwhile, cook the macaroni in a large saucepan of boiling salted water for 8–10 minutes or according to packet instructions until al dente.

Place the mascarpone in a bowl and beat in the mustard, basil, Parmesan and the remaining garlic.

Drain the pasta and return to the pan. Stir in the mascarpone cheese mixture, then carefully fold in the roasted cherry tomatoes along with the prawns. Season with salt and pepper to your taste. Tip into the ovenproof dish that you used for the tomatoes. Bake for 20 minutes until bubbling and golden brown.

To serve, leave the macaroni pie to stand for a few minutes, then serve straight from dish onto warmed plates.

325g (11oz) cherry tomatoes with vines attached

1 garlic clove, peeled and finely chopped

1 tbsp olive oil

350g (12oz) macaroni

250g (9oz) mascarpone cheese

2 tsp Dijon mustard

2 tbsp torn fresh basil leaves

200g (7oz) Parmesan cheese, freshly grated

450g (1lb) peeled Dublin Bay prawns (langoustines), tails and veins removed

salt and freshly ground black pepper

Chicken and Chorizo Rice Bake

300g jar of artichoke hearts in olive oil (or 400g can of artichoke hearts in brine)

25g (1oz) butter

4 chicken breast fillets, with skin on

1 large onion, peeled and finely chopped

2 garlic cloves, peeled and crushed

100g (4oz) raw chorizo sausage, peeled and sliced

350g (12oz) long-grain rice

150ml (5fl oz) dry white wine

600ml (1 pint) chicken stock (see page 215)

2 tbsp roughly chopped fresh flat-leaf parsley

salt and freshly ground black pepper

This one-pot wonder gives maximum flavour with minimum effort and is guaranteed to wake up your taste buds. If you don't have a suitable casserole dish, just use a large sauté pan, then transfer to a roasting tin and cover loosely with foil. Make sure you buy raw chorizo for this dish, which will impart lots of flavour to the rice as it cooks.

Preheat the oven to 180°C (350°F), gas mark 4. Drain the oil from the jar of artichokes and add 1 tablespoon to a casserole dish with a lid. Add half the butter and place on the hob to heat. Season the chicken breasts, add to the dish, skin side down, and cook for 2–3 minutes until lightly browned. Turn over and cook for another minute or so until sealed. Transfer to a plate and set aside.

Add another tablespoon of the drained artichoke oil to the dish together with the remaining butter, then tip in onion and garlic. Sauté for 2–3 minutes until softened but not browned. Add the chorizo and rice and cook for another 2 minutes, stirring regularly until the chorizo has begun to release its oil and all the rice grains are well coated.

Pour the wine into the dish, stirring to combine, then add the stock and fold in the artichokes. Arrange the chicken on top, pushing the breasts down into the rice. Cover with the lid and bake for 35–40 minutes until all the liquid has been absorbed and the chicken and rice are cooked through and tender. Scatter over the parsley and place directly on the table to serve.

sweet things

Pineapple Tarte Tatin

225g (8oz) ready-made puff pastry, thawed if frozen

plain flour, for dusting

1 small, ripe pineapple

100g (4oz) unsalted butter, at room temperature

175g (6oz) caster sugar

clotted cream, to serve

You could also make this tart using apples, plums, peaches or pears – they all work a treat! It can be reheated in the oven for about 15 minutes if you decide to make it in advance but still want to serve it warm.

Preheat the oven to 200°C (400°F), gas mark 6. You need a 25cm (10in) diameter, heavy-based ovenproof frying pan, tarte tatin mould or shallow cake tin (not loose-bottomed). Roll out the pastry on a lightly floured work surface into a circle 5cm (2in) larger in diameter than the pan and about 3mm (⅛in thick) – no thicker than 5mm (¼in) or it will not cook properly. Place the pastry on a baking sheet lined with non-stick parchment paper and chill for at least 30 minutes.

Meanwhile, peel, core and slice the pineapple into rounds. Using a spatula, spread the butter evenly into the pan, mould or tin. Sprinkle over the caster sugar in an even layer, then arrange the pineapple slices in an overlapping layer in the bottom of the pan. Bake for about 5–10 minutes or until the pineapple is caramelised and light golden brown. Remove from the oven and leave to cool.

Lay the chilled pastry sheet over the top of the pineapple, tucking in the edges and turning them down so that when the tart is turned out, the edges create a rim that holds in the caramelised pineapple juices. Bake for 25–30 minutes until the pastry is golden brown and the pineapple slices are completely tender but still holding their shape.

Leave the tart in the pan for a minute or two, then loosen the edges with a round-bladed knife, invert onto a flat plate and use a palette knife to rearrange any pineapple slices that have moved. Leave to cool if time allows, so that all the juices are reabsorbed and the caramel sets slightly. Cut into slices and serve on warmed plates with a dollop of clotted cream.

Peach Open Tartlets
with Fromage Frais Sorbet

Serves 6

These tartlets are really simple. Use firm, ripe peaches when in season or tinned peach halves in natural fruit juice. Layer them up in the pastry base, pop in the oven for just over 10 minutes and voilà! If you don't wish to make the sorbet yourself, shop-bought varieties can work just as well.

If making the sorbet, place the sugar in a heavy-based saucepan with 300ml (10fl oz) of water and bring to the boil. Whisk in the peach yoghurt and fromage frais until well combined, then pour into an ice cream machine and churn following the manufacturer's instructions. Place in the freezer until ready to serve. If you don't have an ice cream machine, you can put the sorbet in a container and pop it in the freezer, then remove and whisk every 25–30 minutes until starting to set.

Preheat the oven to 190°C (375°F), gas mark 5. Unroll the pastry and cut six 10cm (4in) circles, using a large cutter as a template. Prick a few times with a fork, then place on a baking sheet lined with non-stick parchment paper.

Cut the peaches in half and remove the stones. Slice the peach halves very thinly and arrange on the puff pastry rounds in fan-shaped layers, leaving a small border around the edge so that the pastry can rise. Sprinkle evenly with the caster sugar and place a small knob of butter in the centre of each one. Bake for 10–12 minutes or until the pastry is golden brown.

When the peach tartlets are almost ready, heat the apricot jam in a small saucepan or in the microwave on low for 20 seconds. Remove the cooked tartlets from the oven and quickly brush each one with a little of the jam. Arrange on plates and add a scoop of sorbet to each one before serving.

375g (13oz) packet of ready-rolled puff pastry, thawed if frozen

6 small ripe peaches, peeled (or 1 x 400g can peach halves in natural juice)

50g (2oz) caster sugar

50g (2oz) butter, diced

3 tbsp apricot jam

For the sorbet

100g (4oz) caster sugar

150ml (5fl oz) peach yoghurt

200g (7oz) fromage frais

Churros
with Hot Chocolate

Serves 4–6

5 tbsp sunflower oil

1 tbsp ground cinnamon

finely grated rind of 1 lemon

200g (7oz) plain flour

½ tsp salt

1 egg

vegetable oil, for deep-frying

6 tbsp caster sugar

For the hot chocolate

200g (7oz) plain chocolate
(minimum 55% cocoa
solids), broken into squares

900ml (1½ pints) milk

175ml (6fl oz) double cream

Churros are a fried dough snack, originally from Spain, but also popular in mainland Europe and the Americas. The snack gets its name from its shape, which resembles the horns of the Churro breed of sheep originally reared in the grasslands of Spain. They are also sometimes referred to as Spanish or Mexican doughnuts.

To make the churros, place 300ml (10fl oz) of water in a saucepan with the sunflower oil, half the cinnamon and the lemon rind. Bring to the boil. Meanwhile, sieve the flour into a bowl and, once the water mixture is boiling, tip in the flour and salt, beating well with a wooden spoon over a low heat until the mixture leaves the sides of the pan. Leave to cool a little, then beat in the egg.

Melt the plain chocolate in a non-metallic bowl in the microwave on high for 2 minutes or set over a pan of simmering water for 3 minutes.

Heat the vegetable oil in a wok or heavy-based saucepan set over a very high heat, or heat a deep-fat fryer to 180°C (350°F). Spoon the churros mixture into a piping bag fitted with a 2.5cm (1in) star-shaped nozzle. Pipe 7.5cm (3in) lengths directly into the heated oil, using scissors rinsed in warm water to snip off the lengths. Cook for 3–4 minutes until golden, turning once. You may have to do this in batches so as not to overcrowd the pan.

To finish the hot chocolate, place the milk and cream in a small, heavy-based saucepan. Using a spatula, scrape in the melted chocolate, stirring to combine. Heat gently for a few minutes, stirring continuously, until piping hot but not boiling.

Meanwhile, mix together the remaining cinnamon and the sugar on a flat plate. Remove the cooked churros from the oil with a slotted spoon and quickly drain on kitchen paper, then roll in the cinnamon sugar. Pile onto a plate and finish cooking the rest of the churros in the same way. To serve, pour the hot chocolate into mugs or large cappuccino cups and place the plate of churros in the centre of the table so everyone can help themselves.

Summer Fruit Crumble
with Citrus Mascarpone Cream

Serves 4

A classic combination of summer fruits and crumble topping. I love making this in autumn when there are still plenty of fresh berries around. The muscovado sugar gives the crumble a delicious crunchiness.

Preheat the oven to 180°C (350°F), gas mark 4. To prepare the berries, place the sugar in a heavy-based saucepan with the red wine, vanilla seeds, star anise, if using, and lemon juice. Bring to the boil, then reduce the heat and simmer for 5 minutes until slightly thickened and syrup-like. Stir in the berries, remove from the heat and leave to cool.

To make the crumble, place the flour in a bowl and rub in the butter until the mixture resembles fine breadcrumbs. Stir in the sugar, cinnamon, almonds and walnuts until well combined.

Spoon the berry mixture into four individual ovenproof dishes or large ramekins. Sprinkle over the crumble mixture and put the dishes on a baking sheet, then bake for about 20 minutes until the topping is golden brown and bubbling around the edges.

For the citrus cream, beat the mascarpone with the orange, lemon and lime rind and the vanilla seeds. Add enough icing sugar to just sweeten, but so that it isn't *too* sweet. Cover with clingfilm and chill until needed. This will keep in the fridge for up to 3 days.

To make caramel sauce, place the sugar in a heavy-based sauce pan with 120ml (4fl oz) of water. Bring to the boil and cook for about 15 minutes or until golden brown, without stirring; don't let it become too dark or it will taste bitter. Stir in the cream and butter and mix well to combine. Continue to cook until the consistency thickens, stirring occasionally. Use immediately or leave to cool and store in the fridge. This sauce will keep for up to two weeks.

To serve, arrange the summer fruit crumbles on plates, drizzle with the caramel sauce and spoon some of the citrus mascarpone cream on the side. The remainder of the caramel sauce can be served separately in a jug.

100g (4oz) caster sugar

250ml (9fl oz) red wine

½ vanilla pod, split in half and seeds scraped out (retain the remaining pod for citrus marscarpone cream)

2 whole star anise (optional)

1 tbsp freshly squeezed lemon juice

450g (1lb) mixed summer berries (such as strawberries, raspberries, blueberries and blackberries)

For the crumble

175g (6oz) plain flour

100g (4oz) butter

100g (4oz) light muscovado sugar

1 tsp ground cinnamon

50g (2oz) whole blanched almonds, finely chopped

50g (2oz) shelled walnuts, finely chopped

For the citrus mascarpone cream

250g (9oz) mascarpone cheese

finely grated rind of 1 orange, 1 lemon and 1 lime

½ vanilla pod, split in half and seeds scraped out

1–2 tbsp icing sugar, sifted

For the caramel sauce

250g (9oz) caster sugar

225ml (8fl oz) double cream

75g (3oz) butter

Coconut Toasted Meringue
with Lemon Curd Cream and Tropical Fruit

Serves 6

3 egg whites (retain yolks for the lemon curd cream)

175g (6oz) caster sugar

½ vanilla pod, split in half and seeds scraped out (retain remaining pod for the lemon curd cream)

2 tbsp desiccated coconut

2 kiwi fruit, peeled and sliced

1 star fruit, thinly sliced

1 small ripe mango, peeled, stone discarded and sliced

3 passion fruit, halved and pulp scooped out

For the lemon curd cream

2 eggs plus 2 egg yolks (use yolks retained from above)

100g (4oz) caster sugar

½ vanilla pod, split in half and seeds scraped out

finely grated rind and juice of 3 lemons

120g (4½oz) butter, diced

200ml (7fl oz) double cream

This meringue should have a crisp shell and a gooey centre. To achieve this, cook in a very low oven until it has pinkish hue (but don't let it go brown). Decorate with whatever fruit you like, although a tropical selection works particularly well with the sweetness of the meringue.

Preheat the oven to 110°C (225°C), gas mark ¼. Put the egg whites in a bowl and whisk until they are stiff. This is best done with an electric whisk. Gradually add in the caster sugar and vanilla seeds. Continue to whisk until the egg whites become thick and glossy and form stiff peaks (and if you turn the bowl upside down, the mixture doesn't fall out). Fold in half the desiccated coconut. Using a piping bag or palette knife, spread the mixture onto a baking sheet lined with non-stick parchment paper and sprinkle over the remaining coconut. Cook on the lowest shelf of the oven for 1–1½ hours until the meringue is crisp but not browned.

Meanwhile, make the lemon curd cream. Place the eggs and yolks in a heatproof bowl with the sugar and vanilla seeds. Set over a pan of simmering water and whisk until the mixture is pale in colour and holds a figure-of-eight outline made with the whisk. Whisk in the lemon rind and juice and cook for 15–20 minutes until the mixture just starts to set. It is important not to let the water boil under the bowl as this will curdle the eggs in the mixture. Remove the bowl from the heat and leave the curd to cool for 15–20 minutes. Whisk in the diced butter until combined and then leave to cool completely. Place the cream in another bowl and whisk until soft peaks form. Fold into the lemon curd, then cover with clingfilm and chill until needed.

To serve, spread most of the lemon curd cream on the meringue (reserving a couple of tablespoons) and arrange the kiwi slices, star fruit and mango slices on top. Spoon over the passion fruit pulp. To serve, cut into slices and arrange on plates, using small blobs of the reserved lemon curd cream to secure the meringue slices to the plates.

Buttermilk Pannacotta
with Poached Rhubarb

4 gelatine leaves or 1 sachet gelatine powder (see page 208)

400ml (14fl oz) double cream

200ml (7fl oz) buttermilk

100g (4oz) caster sugar

1 vanilla pod, split in half and seeds scraped out

For the poached rhubarb

300ml (10fl oz) red wine

175g (6oz) caster sugar

1 cinnamon stick

½ vanilla pod, split in half and seeds scraped out

1 tsp finely grated fresh root ginger

450g (1lb) rhubarb, washed, trimmed and cut into 7.5cm (3in) pieces, with any thick pieces halved

fresh mint sprigs, to serve

I love to make this with champagne rhubarb, the sweetest rhubarb of all. It appears very early in spring and has slim, tender stalks. The rhubarb can be replaced with plums or strawberries if you prefer and, for a completely different result, try using coconut milk instead of the buttermilk.

If using gelatine leaves, put into a bowl of cold water and leave to soak for 10 minutes. To make the pannacotta, put the cream, buttermilk, caster sugar and scraped-out vanilla seeds into a saucepan and slowly bring up to the boil. Take the pan off the heat, gently squeeze the soaked gelatine leaves dry and add to the pan or, if using powder, whisk into the liquid in a continuous stream. Then whisk continuously until the gelatine has dissolved. Strain the mixture through a sieve into a measuring jug.

Divide the mixture equally between six 150ml (5fl oz) ramekins. Place them on a baking sheet and leave to set in the fridge for at least 3 hours or up to two days.

Meanwhile, prepare the poached rhubarb. Place the red wine in a saucepan with the sugar, cinnamon and vanilla seeds. Pour in 300ml (10fl oz) of water and bring to the boil, then simmer until reduced by half, stirring occasionally.

Add the ginger and rhubarb to the reduced liquid and return to the boil, then reduce the heat and simmer for 3–5 minutes, stirring occasionally, until the rhubarb is just tender. (The cooking time will depend on the ripeness of the rhubarb – it should become soft but still hold its shape.) Stir carefully, to avoid breaking up the rhubarb pieces. Remove from the heat and leave to cool in the juices. The rhubarb keeps very well in the fridge in a sealed container for up to two days.

Unmould the pannacotta by dipping the ramekins briefly into hot water and turning out onto plates. Spoon the poached rhubarb alongside and decorate with mint sprigs to serve.

Catalan Crème Pots

Serves 6–8

This is just one of many great puddings with firm Spanish roots. Very simple to make, it's actually quite light, with all the flavour of the caramel and none of the sticky sweetness. It's similar to the French crème brûlée, except it's not cooked in the oven.

6 egg yolks

100g (4oz) caster sugar

25g (1oz) cornflour

1.2 litres (2 pints) milk

1 cinnamon stick

finely grated rind of 1 lemon and 1 orange

3 tbsp demerara sugar

Place the egg yolks in a heatproof bowl with the caster sugar. Using a hand-held balloon whisk, beat for 5 minutes until thickened. Tip in the cornflour and mix well to combine.

Place the milk in a saucepan with the cinnamon stick, lemon and orange rind. Bring to the boil, then remove from the heat and leave to infuse for 5 minutes.

Strain the milk, discarding the cinnamon stick and the rind, then gradually whisk into the egg and sugar mixture. Place in a clean saucepan and and slowly return to the boil. Reduce the heat and cook gently until the mixture has a thick custard consistency and coats the back of a wooden spoon without running off. Remove from the heat.

Leave to cool, then pour into individual dishes or ramekins and chill for at least 4 hours, or preferably overnight, to allow the crème pots to firm up.

When ready to serve, sprinkle the tops evenly with the demerara sugar and caramelise with a chef's blow torch or under a hot, preheated grill. Put the ramekins onto plates to serve.

Almond and Apricot Tart
with Amaretto Custard

For the pastry

100g (4oz) butter, diced and chilled

175g (6oz) plain flour, sifted plus extra for dusting

pinch of salt

50g (2oz) caster sugar

1 egg yolk

½ tbsp double cream

egg wash (1 full egg with a 1 tbsp milk), for brushing

For the amaretto custard

150ml (5fl oz) double cream

150ml (5fl oz) milk

25g (1oz) ground almonds

½ vanilla pod, split in half and seeds scraped out

2 large egg yolks

1½ tbsp caster sugar

1 tbsp amaretto liqueur

For the almond filling

100g (4oz) butter, at room temperature

100g (4oz) icing sugar

25g (1oz) plain flour

100g (4oz) ground almonds

2 eggs

1 vanilla pod, split in half and seeds scraped out

2 tbsp amaretto liqueur

large pinch of ground cinnamon

400g can of apricot halves in natural juice, drained

2 tbsp apricot jam

1 tbsp toasted flaked almonds

This tart goes beautifully with custard, a classic combination that often gets forgotten about. If you are nervous about the custard curdling, make it in a heatproof bowl set over a pan of simmering water. Put the used vanilla pod into a bag of caster sugar and leave to infuse for a week or so to make vanilla sugar.

To make the pastry, place the butter, flour, salt and sugar in a food processor and blend briefly until the misture resembles breadcrumbs. Add the egg yolk and cream and mix again briefly so that the pastry comes together in a ball. Be careful not to over-work or the pastry will be tough. Cover in clingfilm and chill for 1 hour.

To make the amaretto custard, place the cream and milk in a saucepan with the almonds, vanilla pod and seeds. Bring to scalding point (just before it comes to the boil), remove from the heat and leave to infuse for 15 minutes. Strain into a jug and discard the ground almonds and vanilla pod.

Place the egg yolks and sugar in a bowl, beat until well combined, then slowly pour in the infused cream, stirring continuously to combine. Pour the whole mixture into a clean saucepan and cook for about 10 minutes over a very low heat, stirring continuously, until thickened. Remove from the heat and stir in the amaretto liqueur. Pour into a serving jug and set aside until needed.

Preheat the oven to 180ºC (350ºF), gas mark 4. To make the almond filling, use a hand-held electric whisk to cream the butter and icing sugar together in a large bowl. Add the flour and almonds and gradually beat in the eggs, vanilla, amaretto and cinnamon. Beat for another 5 minutes until light and fluffy.

Roll out the pastry on a lightly floured work surface and use it to line a 23cm (9in) fluted, loose-bottomed flan tin. Cover with foil, then fill with baking beans and bake 'blind' for about 20 minutes until the pastry is golden brown. Remove from the oven; discard the baking beans and the foil and brush the warm pastry case ◗

with egg wash. Spread the almond filling in the bottom of the pastry base and carefully arrange the apricot halves on top, gently pressing them down onto the filling.

Bake the tart for 25–30 minutes until cooked through and golden brown on top. Warm the jam in a small saucepan or in the microwave for 20 seconds on low and use to brush over the tart, then sprinkle with the toasted almonds. Cut the tart into slices and arrange on plates. Serve with the jug of amaretto custard.

Coconut Pearls in Coconut Milk
with Caramelised Bananas

Serves 4

I first tasted this dessert in Sapa, North Vietnam-where it is traditionally served with slices of fresh, ripe mango instead of the bananas I've used here. It reminds me of desserts my mum used to make for us when we were little. Needless to say, I was hooked immediately!

Preheat the oven to 180°C (350°F), gas mark 4. Place the coconut milk in a large saucepan with the vanilla seeds (saving the pod for later), sugar and 250ml (9fl oz) of water and simmer gently until the sugar dissolves, stirring occasionally. Reduce the heat to very low, add the tapicoa and simmer for 10 minutes, stirring constantly. Stir in the lime rind and cook for another 10–15 minutes until the tapioca is just cooked and translucent. In the final few minutes of cooking stir in the double cream. Remove from the heat and keep warm.

To make the caramel for the bananas, place 100ml (3½fl oz) of cold water in a small, heavy-based saucepan with the caster sugar. Bring to the boil, stirring occasionally, until the sugar has dissolved, then simmer for about 15 minutes until you have achieved a golden-brown caramel (140°C/275°F if using a sugar thermometer).

When the caramel is golden brown, carefully add the rum and simmer for 1 minute. Then add the orange juice and the reserved vanilla pod. The sugar will become lumpy at first but do n't worry, simply return to a low heat for 5 minutes and stir gently until you have achieved a smooth consistency.

Peel the bananas and cut in half lengthways. Melt the butter in a frying pan and add the bananas cut-side down. Pan-fry for 1 minute, being careful not to break them. Once they are soft, pour over the orange and rum caramel and simmer for 2–3 minutes until the bananas are golden brown.

To serve, ladle the coconut pearls into serving bowls or glasses and carefully arrange two pieces of banana on each one. Sprinkle over the toasted sesame seeds and decorate with the mint sprigs.

2 x 400ml cans of coconut milk

1 vanilla pod, split in half and seeds scraped out

175g (6oz) caster sugar

75g (3oz) tapioca pearls, rinsed and drained

finely grated rind of 1 lime

150ml (5fl oz) double cream

4 tsp toasted sesame seeds

4 fresh mint sprigs, to decorate

For the caramelised bananas

40g (1½oz) caster sugar

1 tbsp dark rum

150ml (5fl oz) freshly squeezed orange juice, strained

2 ripe bananas

25g (1oz) butter

4 small scoops of vanilla ice cream, to serve

Coconut Crème Caramel
with Malibu and Pineapple

Serves 8

400ml can of coconut milk

100ml (3½fl oz) double cream

1 vanilla pod, split in half and seeds scraped out

4 eggs, plus 3 egg yolks

100g (4oz) caster sugar

whipped cream, to serve

1 tbsp chopped fresh mint, plus extra sprigs to garnish

For the caramel

150g (5oz) caster sugar

100ml (3½fl oz) Malibu (coconut liqueur)

sunflower oil, for greasing

For the pineapple compote

50g (2oz) caster sugar

100ml (3½fl oz) Malibu (coconut liqueur)

1 small pineapple, peeled, cored and diced

Experiment freely with different liqueurs and tropical fruit – try Cointreau with mango or triple sec with papaya, for instance. The crème caramels are much easier to un-mould when they have been left overnight to give the syrup a chance to settle.

First make the caramel. Place the caster sugar in a small, heavy-based saucepan with 50ml (2fl oz) of water. Bring to the boil, stirring until the sugar has dissolved. Reduce the heat and continue to cook, without stirring, for about 10 minutes. When the sauce is a deep golden brown, pour 100ml (3½fl oz) of water into the hot caramel to stop it from browning further and burning. The sauce will be very hot, so be careful. Stir in the Malibu and return to the heat until the caramel has a thick, syrup-like consistency. Lightly oil ramekins or small teacups and divide the caramel between them. Set aside.

Preheat the oven to 140°C (275°F), gas mark 1. Place the coconut milk in a heavy-based saucepan with the cream and vanilla pod. Bring to the boil and then keep warm. Whisk the eggs in a large bowl with the extra yolks, caster sugar and vanilla seeds. Pour the hot milk mixture onto the egg mixture. Whisk until combined, then pass through a sieve into a jug. Carefully pour into the ramekins right up to the rim.

Place the ramekins in a roasting tin and half fill the tin with boiling water (this is called a 'bain-marie'). Cover the tin with foil to keep in the heat and place the roasting tin in the oven for 30–40 minutes or until the crème caramels are set. The mixture will still be slightly wobbly. Leave the ramekins in the tin to cool, then transfer them to the fridge until ready to serve. They will sit happily in the fridge covered in clingfilm for up to two days.

To make the pineapple compote, place the sugar, Malibu and 100ml (3½fl oz) of water in a saucepan and bring to the boil, stirring until the sugar has dissolved. Add the diced pineapple and bring back to boiling point, then remove from heat and leave to cool completely. Pour into a non-metallic bowl and stir in the mint. Cover with clingfilm and chill until needed. ◗

To serve, turn the crème caramels out of the ramekins onto chilled plates, spooning over any caramel that remains in the ramekins. Spoon the pineapple compote around them, add a dollop of whipped cream to the side and garnish with a mint sprig.

Pear Belle-Hélène

This classic dessert was invented by the famous French chef Escoffier. He was inspired by Jacques Offenbach's 1864 operetta La Belle Hélène. I'll never forget the first time I tasted it, while working in the Grand Hotel in Berlin – I just kept going back for more!

Place the pear halves in a saucepan with the apple juice, sugar, orange slices, cinnamon stick, vanilla pod and star anise, if using. Bring to the boil, then reduce the heat and simmer for 15–20 minutes until the pear halves are tender. Remove from the heat and leave to cool in the syrup. Remove the cooled pears with a slotted spoon.

To make the mousse, melt the chocolate in a heatproof bowl over a saucepan of simmering water. In another bowl set over simmering water, whisk the eggs with the Baileys and 2 tablespoons of cold water until double in size. Do not allow the water in the pan to boil or the eggs will cook.

Fold the melted chocolate into the egg mixture, then leave to cool for 5 minutes. Meanwhile, whisk the cream in a bowl, then fold into the chocolate mousse. Cover with clingfilm and chill for 2–3 hours, or overnight.

To make the chocolate fudge, melt the chocolate gently in a heat-proof bowl set over a saucepan of slowly simmering water. Set aside. Place the cream in a separate pan with the caster sugar and butter. Bring to a simmer, stirring until the sugar has dissolved.

Remove the cream mixture from the heat and leave to cool a little, then whisk in the melted chocolate until you achieve a smooth sauce. Pour into a jug and cover with clingfilm. This sauce keeps very well in the fridge and can be warmed gently when needed.

To serve, put a dollop of chocolate mousse onto each serving plate. Remove the centre cores from the pears and carefully slice each half into a fan. Place two beside each portion of mousse. Drizzle some of the chocolate fudge sauce over the fanned-out pears. Sprinkle with toasted almonds, if desired.

6 ripe Conference pears, peeled and halved

300ml (10fl oz) apple juice

50g (2oz) caster sugar

1 orange, sliced with peel on

1 cinnamon stick

½ vanilla pod, cut in half lengthways

2 whole star anise (optional)

50g (2oz) toasted flaked almonds (optional)

For the chocolate mousse

225g (8oz) plain chocolate (minimum 55% cocoa solids), broken into squares

3 eggs

2 tbsp Baileys Irish Cream liqueur

300ml (10fl oz) double cream

For the chocolate fudge sauce

350g (12oz) plain chocolate (minimum 55% cocoa solids), broken into squares

300ml (10fl oz) double cream

75g (3oz) caster sugar

50g (2oz) unsalted butter

Serves 6–8

Lemon and Mango Cheesecake

For the biscuit base

75g (3oz) butter, plus extra for greasing

250g (9oz) gingernut biscuits, crushed

For the filling

4 gelatine leaves or 1 sachet gelatine powder

175ml (6fl oz) milk

1 vanilla pod, split in half and seeds removed

175g (6oz) caster sugar

2 x 250g (9oz) tubs of mascarpone cheese

finely grated rind and juice of 2 lemons

150ml (5fl oz) thick Greek yoghurt

For the fruit topping

2 gelatine leaves

400g can of mango slices in natural juice, drained (or 2 large fresh mangoes, peeled, stones discarded and sliced)

fresh raspberries, to serve

I've used gelatine leaves in this recipe but you could use powdered gelatine if you prefer. It is sold in sachets of 11g (²/₅oz, 3 level teaspoons), which is enough to set this cheesecake; simply follow the instructions on the packet.

To make the base, lightly butter a 23cm (9 in) loose-bottomed, spring-form cake tin. Melt the butter in a saucepan set over a gentle heat or in a bowl in the microwave. Add the crushed gingernuts and mix well. Spread the mixture evenly over the base of the tin, pressing down with the back of a spoon to flatten. Place in the fridge to chill for at least 10 minutes or up to 24 hours.

To make the filling, soak the gelatine leaves in a bowl of cold water for 10 minutes. Place the milk in a saucepan set over a medium heat and add the vanilla seeds, whisking to combine. Cook until it just reaches boiling point, but do not allow to boil. Remove the gelatine leaves from the water and gently squeeze out the excess moisture. Add to the pan along with the sugar and whisk until dissolved. Pour into a large bowl and leave to cool a little.

Beat the mascarpone cheese into the cooled milk mixture along with the lemon rind and juice, then stir in the yoghurt. Pour on top of the set biscuit base and chill for at least 1 hour until set.

To make the topping, soak the gelatine leaves in a bowl of cold water for 10 minutes. Place the mango slices in a food processor and blend until smooth. Heat a tablespoon of water in a small saucepan or in the microwave. Gently squeeze the gelatine dry and stir into the hot water until dissolved. Add the mango purée and pour over the set cheesecake filling, spreading evenly with the back of a spoon. Chill for another 2–3 hours until set.

To serve, remove the cheesecake from the tin and transfer to a serving plate. Cut into slices and arrange on plates with some fresh raspberries.

larder

Beef Stock

450g (1lb) shin of beef, cut into pieces

450g (1lb) marrow bones or knuckle of veal, chopped

1 tbsp olive oil

1 onion, peeled and chopped

1 carrot, peeled and chopped

1 celery stick, chopped

1 tbsp tomato purée

150ml (5fl oz) red wine

1 small garlic bulb, halved crossways

1 bouquet garni (fresh parsley stalks, sprigs of thyme and a bay leaf tied together)

½ tsp salt

This stock takes a little while to make but it's worthwhile, as you'll find plenty of opportunities to use it. It is important to use red wine and tomato purée for real depth of colour. The stock will of course store very well in the fridge for 3–4 days and in the freezer for up to six months. Ask your local butcher for the bones – they should have plenty.

Preheat the oven to 220°C (425°F), gas mark 7. Place the shin of beef and marrow bones or knuckle of veal in a roasting tin and cook in the oven for 30–40 minutes or until well browned.

Meanwhile, heat the oil in a large saucepan until very hot. Add the onion, carrot and celery and sauté for about 5 minutes until just beginning to colour. Stir in the tomato purée, then pour in the red wine and allow to simmer and reduce.

Add the roasted meat bones to the vegetable and wine mixture along with the garlic and bouquet garni. Season with the salt and pour in 1.75 litres (3 pints) of water. Bring to the boil and skim off any fat or scum, then partially cover with a lid and simmer for 4–5 hours until you have achieved a well-flavoured stock.

Strain the stock and once it is cold remove any trace of fat from the surface with a large spoon. Use as required or freeze in 600ml (1 pint) cartons or ice cream tubs, and defrost as and when you need it. You could also freeze the stock in ice cube bags for small quantities to add to your cooking – just be careful not to drop one into your gin and tonic by mistake!

Vegetable Stock

If time allows, I like to allow my vegetable stock to marinate for two days so that the flavours can really infuse and develop. This creates a fuller taste and is definitely worth the wait. I've included star anise, which is a very fragrant spice and is available from most major supermarkets.

Place all of the ingredients in a large saucepan and cover with 1.75 litres (3 pints) of water. Bring to a simmer, then cook without a lid for another 30 minutes until the vegetables are tender.

Either set aside to marinate for two days in a cool place, or if you're short of time, use immediately. Strain the stock and taste; if you find the flavour is not full enough, return to the pan and reduce until you are happy. Use as required, keep in the fridge for 3–4 days, or freeze in 600ml (1 pint) cartons, ice cream tubs or ice cube bags, and defrost when you need it.

2 leeks, trimmed and finely chopped

2 onions, peeled and finely chopped

2 carrots, peeled and cut into 1cm (½in) dice

2 celery sticks, finely chopped

1 fennel bulb, cut into 1cm (½in) dice

1 head garlic, sliced in half crossways

200ml (7 fl oz) white wine

1 fresh thyme sprig

1 bay leaf

1 tsp coriander seeds

1 star anise

1 tsp pink peppercorns

pinch of salt

Chicken Stock

I use chicken stock more than any other type, as it makes the perfect base for soups, stews and sauces. It freezes very well and so I always try to make a batch when we've had a roast chicken for dinner.

Place the chicken carcass in a large saucepan and cover with 1.75 litres (3 pints) of water. Bring to the boil, then skim off any fat and scum from the surface. Reduce the heat to a simmer and tip in all the remaining ingredients.

Simmer gently for another 2–3 hours, skimming occasionally and tasting regularly to check the flavour. When you are happy with it, remove from the heat and sieve the stock. Leave to cool and remove any fat that settles on the top, then use as required, keep in the fridge for 3–4 days, or freeze in 600ml (1 pint) cartons, ice cream tubs or ice cube bags and defrost when you need it.

1 large chicken carcass, skin and fat removed and chopped

2 leeks, trimmed and chopped

2 onions, peeled and chopped

2 carrots, peeled and chopped

2 celery sticks, chopped

1 fresh thyme sprig

1 bay leaf

handful fresh parsley stalks

1 tsp white peppercorns

pinch of salt

Five-spice Balsamic Cream

Makes about 300ml (10fl oz)

We use a lot of this in our restaurant kitchen. It goes perfectly with beef, chicken or fish, and is lovely drizzled over scallops or prawns.

150ml (5fl oz) double cream

150ml (5fl oz) beef stock (see page 212)

1 tsp Chinese five-spice powder

1 tbsp tomato purée

2 tbsp balsamic vinegar

salt and freshly ground black pepper

Place the cream in a saucepan with the stock, five-spice, tomato purée and balsamic vinegar. Bring to the boil, then reduce the heat and simmer for about 5 minutes until reduced and thickened.

Season to taste and keep warm or leave to cool completely, then transfer to a bowl and cover with clingfilm. This can be stored in the fridge for up to three days and reheated as needed.

Infused Oils

Making flavoured oils is easy, and the end product adds a great deal to your cooking. Use them instead of spices and herbs, or to flavour vegetables and meats. Infused oils make great bases for salad dressings, marinades and sauces. Bottles of infused oils look great on kitchen shelves, and are always an original gift.

The technique for making infused oil is much the same whether the ingredient is basil, rosemary, oregano, garlic, chillies, mushrooms or citrus fruit. For every 225ml (8fl oz) of olive oil, use 100g (4oz) of fresh basil leaves or any other soft-leaved green herb, such as chervil, chives, coriander or mint. Tarragon does not work well, except early in the spring when it is very sweet, as it tends to taste bitter when infused.

Bring a large saucepan of water to a boil. Add the herbs, making sure that the leaves are submerged, and leave for 5 seconds. Drain into a strainer and immediately plunge the herbs into a bowl of iced water. Drain well and squeeze out all the liquid. Purée in a blender with olive oil. Strain the purée immediately through a fine-mesh strainer. Strain again through four layers of cheesecloth (or use brand new J Cloths). Place in a sterilised glass bottle, cover tightly and chill. Use within one week for the best flavour.

Chilli oil is even easier to make and all you need to do is to pop two dried red chillies into a saucepan containing 225ml (8fl oz) of olive oil and warm gently for about 5 minutes to allow the flavours to infuse. Leave until completely cool before transferring to a sterilised glass bottle and use within two months of opening. You can use the infused oil in vinaigrette or simply drizzled over a tomato salad with a splash of balsamic vinegar. It is also excellent as a marinade ingredient for chicken, fish or Mediterranean vegetables.

Acknowledgements

This has been a fun book to write. It brought back so many memories of happy holidays and sunny days filming. Once again it was a pleasure to work with Orla Broderick in compiling the recipes.

My film crew Billy Keady and Ray deBrún are the best fed in the business! They, along with producer David Hare, did a great job on the television series. As did food stylist Sharon Hearne-Smith, production manager Sally Walker, and production assistant Aina Tortella. Anna Skidmore and Bartomeu Dèya of the Mallorca Tourist Board were very helpful to us. Thank you also to Brian Walsh of RTE who believed in the project from the start.

Back home I have the good fortune to have a dedicated, talented and hard working team. Thank you to head chef Glen Wheeler, and chefs Declan Greene and Vicky Boughton, to restaurant manager Bláithín McCabe and to all of my staff at MacNean House and Restaurant. Blacklion is where my heart stays.

I have wonderful suppliers who provide excellent produce. Thank you to my butcher, Kevin McGovern; Ken Moffitt who supplies my free range poultry; Mark at Kettle Foods; Peter Curry for his seafood; McDaids for their fresh Irish fruit and vegetables; Paul, Samantha, Declan and Hugh at B.D. Foods in Monaghan; Rod at Eden Plants in Co. Leitrim; and Ernst of Barbizon Herbs. With such good ingredients it is hard to go wrong.

A special thank you to our customers, many of whom travel to dine with us. It means so much that you enjoy our food.

Throughout the year I get marvellous support at my demonstrations from Eoin O'Flynn and John Martin of Flogas. I eat up the miles but they are made very comfortable by Tom O'Connor, Louise Collins and Anna Dawson at VW Group Ireland.

Agri Aware have provided me with an educational role which I value. It is a pleasure to have the opportunity to encourage young people to eat well and to see them learn to cook. Thank you to James Kelly, Mairead Lavery, Ciara O'Kelly and Conor Keppel and continued success in your work.

This year I was honoured to be asked by our Tánaiste, Mary Coughlan, T.D. to join the board of Safefood. It has been a valuable learning experience working with Martin Higgins and his team.

I get great satisfaction from my work with Dunnes Stores. Thank you to Margaret, Michael and Anne Heffernan and Dick Reeves and their first class food team.

I have received consistent support from many broadcasters and journalists. Marian Finucane and her team Anne Farrell and Elaine Conlon have been so good to me. It seems that everybody listens to Marian. Thank you also to Aoife Byrne and Suzanne Byrne of the RTE Guide. My colleagues that go back to my Open House days, Mary Kennedy and Marty Whelan, always remember me. Big stars and firm friends. I have also been encouraged by kind words from Georgina Campbell, Paolo Tullio, Tom Doorly, John McKenna, Ross Golden Bannon and Kevin Flanagan.

That all this happens is due to my tireless publicist, Mary Tallent. Thank you Mary for your flair and constant good humour, and also your colleagues at Purcell Masterson in Kilkenny, Naoimh Murphy, Orla Nolan and John Purcell.

This book came about because of a meeting of minds. My agent, John Masterson, wants only the best for me. Jenny Heller of HarperCollins is just that. A huge thank you to Jenny for her belief in me and to her fantastic colleagues at HarperCollins, Ione Walder, Charlotte Allen and Moira Reilly. And to David Munns for his fabulous photography, Nicky Barneby for the beautiful design and Anna Martin for creating the cover. It has been a privilege to work with you all.

Finally, my mother Vera is my inspiration. My family are always there for me and don't expect any thanks for it. There is no greater joy than to cook for you all together. Thank you so much.

Picture Credits: All photography © David Munns except for **p2-3** © Shutterstock/ Inacio Pires; **p14** © iStockphoto.com/ Linda Steward; **p34-35** © Shutterstock/ Vera Bogaerts; **p50** © iStockphoto.com/ Ismail Egler; **p58-59** © iStockphoto.com/ Heinz Linke; **p79** © Shutterstock/ afotoshop; **p92** © iStockphoto.com/ Mike Dabell; **p96** © iStockphoto.com/ Almar Joling; **p99** © Shutterstock/ Dafne; **p106** © Shutterstock / Marcin-linfernum; **p108-109** © iStockphoto.com/ Rachel Dewis; **p117** © Shutterstock/ Noam Armonn; **p136-137** © Shutterstock/ Stefan Ataman; **p176** © Shutterstock/ Mario Bruno; **p216** © Shutterstock/ Aleksandr Frolov.

Index

almonds: almond and apricot tart
200–1
    spiced glazed almonds 33
amaretto custard 200–1
anchovies: salad Niçoise 112
apricots: almond and apricot tart
200–1
    apricot relish 143
artichoke hearts: artichoke and
Parmesan purée 18
    chicken and chorizo rice bake 182
    porcini and artichoke pasta 162
Asian pork burger 62
asparagus: griddled asparagus with
roasted red peppers 130–1
    Parma ham-wrapped 18
aubergines: aubergine and
mozzarella parcels 26
    aubergine chutney 90
    baked Mediterranean veg 135
    oven-baked tomatoes with
ratatouille 129
    roasted aubergine and cumin soup
19
    roasted stuffed aubergines 127
    turkey moussaka 36–7
avocados: avocado hummus 13
    blackened chicken with roasted
red pepper and avocado salsa
41
    grilled salmon with 89

bacon: roasted haddock with
smoked bacon 98
balsamic cream, five-spice 217
bananas, caramelised 203
bean sprouts: Vietnamese beef
noodle soup 81
beef: chargrilled Thai beef salad 116
    chilli cornbread pie 67
    grilled rib-eye steak with smoked
paprika and red pepper butter
63
    inverted Cashel Blue burger 61
    stock 212
    Vietnamese beef noodle soup 81
beetroot carpaccio with creamed

goat's cheese 132
black bean sauce 23
black cod with a sweet basil crust
84
blackened chicken 41
brandade, smoked salmon 94
bread: bruschetta platter 17–18
    chargrilled vegetable layered
sandwich 120
    flatbread 124
broad beans: chicken and broad
bean paella 42
bruschetta platter 17–18
bulgar wheat: tabbouleh salad 161
burgers: Asian pork burger 62
    inverted Cashel Blue burger 61
    lamb and mint burger 62
butterflied lamb 74
butterflied poussin 48
buttermilk pannacotta 198
butternut squash, crispy pancetta
and pine nut pasta 174

cake, orange polenta, 191
cannellini beans: Italian bean salad
118
    oven-roasted 173
caramel: caramel sauce 195
    caramelised bananas 203
    caramelised pork belly 70–1
    Catalan cream pots 199
    coconut crème caramel 204–5
carrots: spicy root vegetables 169
Catalan cream pots 199
cauliflower: seared scallops with
curried cauliflower purée 86–7
cheese: artichoke and Parmesan
purée 18
    aubergine and mozzarella parcels
26
    baked eggs with tomatoes, chorizo
and Manchego cheese 148
    baked macaroni pie with Dublin
Bay prawns 181
    baked Mediterranean vegetables
135
    chunky Greek salad with feta

cheese 111
    crispy wild mushroom risotto balls
179–80
    garlic yoghurt cheese 140
    Gorgonzola, pear and rocket salad
110
    halloumi with griddled pitta 15
    inverted Cashel Blue burger 61
    mozzarella fritters 150
    onion tart with mozzarella 154
    Parma-wrapped pork fillet stuffed
with pesto 72
    pizza Brie tart 145
    quick quesadillas 144
    roasted butternut squash, crispy
pancetta and pine nut pasta
174
    roasted Piedmont peppers with
feta cheese 119
    shallot tarte tatin 122
    Swiss chard and ricotta ravioli 164
    turkey moussaka 36–7
    twice-baked cheese soufflé 149
    see also goat's cheese
cheesecake, lemon and mango 208
chicken: blackened chicken with
roasted red pepper and
avocado salsa 41
    butterflied poussin 48
    chicken and broad bean paella 42
    chicken and chorizo rice bake 182
    chicken and wild mushroom
wontons 23–4
    chicken satay 28
    creamy chicken korma 47
    harissa roast chicken 57
    Singapore noodles 167
    spicy chicken mango noodles 38
    stock 215
    Thai yellow chicken curry 52
    Vietnamese-style grilled five-spice
chicken thigh salad 51
chickpeas: avocado hummus 13
    pumpkin, spinach and chickpea
curry 124
    roasted red pepper and chilli
hummus 12

chillies: chargrilled Thai beef 116
  chilli cornbread pie 67
  chilli jam 107
  chilli salsa 144
  roasted red pepper and chilli
      hummus 12
  turkey enchiladas with chilli sauce
      56
chocolate: churros with hot
      chocolate 188
  pear Belle-Hélène 207
chorizo: baked eggs with tomatoes,
      chorizo and Manchego cheese
      148
  chicken and chorizo rice bake 182
churros with hot chocolate 188
chutney, aubergine 90
citrus mascarpone cream 195
clams: chicken and broad bean
      paella 42
  hake with clams, fennel and cherry
      tomatoes 100
coconut milk: coconut crème
      caramel 204–5
  coconut pearls in 203
  monkfish in Thai yellow curry broth
      104
coconut toasted meringue 196
cod: black cod with a sweet basil
      crust 84
cornbread pie, chilli 67
courgettes: baked Mediterranean
      vegetables 135
  oven-baked tomatoes with
      ratatouille 129
  pizza Brie tart 145
couscous: lemon and herb 169
  Moroccan lamb tagine 64
crab: seafood lasagne 171–2
  warm crab and spinach tart 153–4
cream: buttermilk pannacotta 198
  five-spice balsamic cream 217
cream pots, Catalan 199
crème caramel, coconut 204–5
crudités, garlic yoghurt cheese with
      140
crumble, summer fruit 195
cucumber: pickled cucumber salad
      28
curries: creamy chicken korma 47
  curried mayonnaise 107
  lamb rogan josh 75
  monkfish in Thai yellow curry broth
      104
  pumpkin, spinach and chickpea
      curry 124

Thai green prawn curry 53
Thai red duck curry 53
Thai yellow chicken curry 52
custard, amaretto 200–1

dates: Moroccan lamb tagine 64
  seared scallops with date jam 86–7
Dublin Bay prawns: baked macaroni
      pie with 181
  oven-roasted 10
  seafood lasagne 171–2
  Thai green prawn curry 53
  Vietnamese spring rolls 25
duck: crispy shredded Chinese duck
      salad 54
  tea-smoked Barbary duck 45
  Thai red duck curry 53

eel: smoked fish platter 94
eggs: baked eggs with tomatoes,
      chorizo and Manchego cheese
      148
  Greek-style omelette 155
  huevos rancheros 138
  pancetta frittata 155
  salad Niçoise 112
enchiladas, turkey 56

fig and onion marmalade 17
fish see cod, tuna etc
five-spice balsamic cream 217
flatbread 124
French beans: salad Niçoise 112
frittata, pancetta 155
fritters: churros 188
  mozzarella fritters 150
fromage frais sorbet 187
fruit: coconut toasted meringue with
      tropical fruit 196
  summer fruit crumble 195
  see also bananas, pineapple etc

garlic yoghurt cheese 140
goat's cheese: beetroot carpaccio
      with 132
  goat's cheese pâté 143
  goat's cheese with fig and onion
      marmalade 17
  roasted stuffed aubergines with
      127
Gorgonzola, pear and rocket salad
      110
Greek salad, chunky 111
Greek-style omelette 155
haddock with smoked bacon, haricot
      bean purée and wilted spinach

98
hake with clams, fennel and cherry
      tomatoes 100
halloumi with griddled pitta 15
ham see Parma ham
haricot beans: red onion, bean and
      tomato salad 15
  roasted haddock with 98
harissa: crispy fried squid with 20
  harissa roast chicken 57
huevos rancheros 138
hummus: avocado 13
  roasted red pepper and chilli 12

Italian bean salad 118

lamb: butterflied lamb with spiced
      mint and yoghurt rub 74
  lamb and mint burger 62
  lamb rogan josh 75
  lamb shanks osso bucco 68
  Moroccan lamb tagine 64
  rack of lamb with tapenade toasts
      and wilted spinach 76–7
langoustines see Dublin Bay prawns
lasagne, seafood 171–2
lemon: coconut toasted meringue
      with lemon curd cream 196
  lemon and herb couscous 169
  lemon and mango cheesecake 208
lentils: mackerel with Puy lentils 85
  Puy lentil, red onion and sun-dried
      tomato salad 163

macaroni pie with Dublin Bay prawns
      181
mackerel: mackerel with Puy lentils
      and sherry vinaigrette 85
  smoked fish platter 94
mangoes: lemon and mango
      cheesecake 208
  spicy chicken and mango noodles
      38
mascarpone cream, citrus 195
mayonnaise, curried 107
meringue, coconut toasted 196
monkfish in Thai yellow curry broth
      104
Moroccan lamb tagine 64
moussaka, turkey 36–7
mozzarella fritters 150
mushrooms: chicken and wild
      mushroom wontons 23–4
  crispy wild mushroom risotto balls
      179–80
  pizza Brie tart 145

porcini and artichoke pasta 162
stir-fried baby pak choi with 128
mussel and saffron risotto 177

noodles: Singapore noodles 167
spicy chicken and mango noodles 38
Vietnamese beef noodle soup 81
Vietnamese spring rolls 25

oils, infused 219
olives: baked sea bass with tomatoes and 88
marinated olives 33
Parma ham wrapped asparagus with tapenade 18
rack of lamb with tapenade toasts 76–7
salad Niçoise 112
omelette, Greek-style 155
onions: goat's cheese with fig and onion marmalade 17
Italian bean salad with griddled red onion 118
onion tart with mozzarella and semi-sun dried tomatoes 154
Puy lentil, red onion and sun-dried tomato salad 163
red onion, bean and tomato salad 15
oranges: orange polenta cake 191
pomegranate, orange and mint salad 115
oysters with spinach and lemongrass 30

paella, chicken and broad bean 42
pak choi: stir-fried baby pak choi with mushrooms 128
pancetta: pancetta frittata 155
roasted butternut squash, crispy pancetta and pine nut pasta 174
pannacotta, buttermilk 198
Parma ham: Parma ham wrapped asparagus 18
Parma-wrapped pork fillet 72
parsley: salsa verde 103
tabbouleh salad 161
parsnips: spicy root vegetables 169
passionfruit tart 192
pasta: baked macaroni pie with Dublin Bay prawns 181
porcini and artichoke pasta 162
roasted butternut squash, crispy pancetta and pine nut pasta 174
seafood lasagne 171–2

smoked salmon and saffron orzo 158
patatas bravas, cracked 27
pâté, goat's cheese 143
peach open tartlets 187
peanut butter: chicken satay 28
pears: Gorgonzola, pear and rocket salad 110
pear Belle-Hélène 207
peppers: baked Mediterranean vegetables 135
blackened chicken with roasted red pepper and avocado salsa 41
griddled asparagus with roasted red peppers and Parmesan 130–1
huevos rancheros 138
oven-baked tomatoes with ratatouille 129
roasted Piedmont peppers with feta cheese 119
roasted red pepper and chilli hummus 12
roasted red pepper and tomato sauce 150
seared tuna with sweetcorn, red pepper and lime salsa 93
smoked paprika and red pepper butter 63
turkey enchiladas 56
pesto, Parma-wrapped pork fillet stuffed with 72
pickled cucumber salad 28
pine nuts: Parma-wrapped pork fillet stuffed with pesto 72
roasted butternut squash, crispy pancetta and pine nut pasta 174
pineapple: coconut crème caramel with 204–5
pineapple tarte tatin 186
pitta, halloumi with griddled 15
pizza Brie tart 145
plum sauce 25
polenta cake, orange 191
pomegranate, orange and mint salad 115
porchetta with sautéed potatoes 78
porcini and artichoke pasta 162
pork: Asian pork burger 62
barbecued brine pork chops 69
caramelised pork belly with mustard potato purée 70–1
Parma-wrapped pork fillet stuffed with pesto 72
porchetta with sautéed potatoes

78
potatoes: cracked patatas bravas 27
mustard potato purée 70–1
porchetta with sautéed potatoes 78
salad Niçoise 112
smoked salmon brandade 94
poussin, butterflied 48
prawns: Singapore noodles 167
Thai green prawn curry 53
Vietnamese spring rolls 25
see also Dublin Bay prawns
pumpkin, spinach and chickpea curry 124
Puy lentil, red onion and sun-dried tomato salad 163

quesadillas with chilli salsa 144

raspberry sauce 192
ratatouille, oven-baked tomatoes with 129
ravioli, Swiss chard and ricotta 164
red kidney beans: chilli cornbread pie 67
relish, apricot 143
rhubarb, buttermilk pannacotta with 198
rice: chicken and broad bean paella 42
chicken and chorizo rice bake 182
crispy wild mushroom risotto balls 179–80
mussel and saffron risotto 177
risotto: crispy wild mushroom risotto balls 179–80
mussel and saffron risotto 177
rocket: Gorgonzola, pear and rocket salad 110
root vegetables, spicy 169

salads: chargrilled Thai beef 116
chunky Greek salad 111
crispy shredded Chinese duck salad 54
Gorgonzola, pear and rocket salad 110
Italian bean salad 118
pickled cucumber salad 28
salads (cont.)
pomegranate, orange and mint salad 115
Puy lentil, red onion and sun-dried tomato salad 163
red onion, bean and tomato salad

15

salad Niçoise 112

spicy chicken and mango noodles 38

tabbouleh salad 161

Vietnamese-style grilled five-spice chicken thigh salad 51

salmon: grilled salmon with avocado and sun-dried tomato dressing 89

seafood lasagne with salmon mousse 171–2

salsa: chilli salsa 144

roasted red pepper and avocado salsa 41

salsa verde 103

sweetcorn, red pepper and lime salsa 93

sardines, fried butterflied 90

scallops with date jam and curried cauliflower purée 86–7

sea bass with tomatoes and olives 88

seafood see prawns, scallops etc

seafood lasagne 171–2

shallot tarte tatin 122

sherry vinaigrette 85

Singapore noodles 167

smoked fish platter 94

smoked salmon: smoked salmon and saffron orzo 158

smoked salmon brandade 94

sole: crispy lemon sole with chilli jam 107

sorbet, fromage frais 187

soufflé, twice-baked cheese 149

soups: roasted aubergine and cumin soup 19

Vietnamese beef noodle soup 81

spinach: poached oysters with lemongrass and 30

pumpkin, spinach and chickpea curry 124

rack of lamb with wilted spinach 76–7

roasted haddock with smoked bacon and wilted spinach 98

warm crab and spinach tart 153–4

spring rolls, Vietnamese 25

squash: roasted butternut squash, crispy pancetta and pine nut pasta 174

squid, crispy fried 20

steak, grilled rib-eye 63

stock 212–15

summer fruit crumble 195

sweet potatoes, harissa roast chicken with 57

sweetcorn, red pepper and lime salsa 93

Swiss chard and ricotta ravioli 164

swordfish with salsa verde 103

tabbouleh salad 161

tagine, Moroccan lamb 64

tapenade: chargrilled vegetable layered sandwich with 120

Parma ham wrapped asparagus with 18

rack of lamb with tapenade toasts 76–7

tapioca: coconut pearls 203

tarts: almond and apricot tart 200–1

onion tart with mozzarella 154

passionfruit tart 192

peach open tartlets 187

pineapple tarte tatin 186

pizza Brie tart 145

shallot tarte tatin 122

warm crab and spinach tart 153–4

tea-smoked Barbary duck 45

Thai green prawn curry 53

Thai red duck curry 53

Thai yellow chicken curry 52

tomatoes: baked eggs with tomatoes, chorizo and Manchego cheese 148

baked Mediterranean vegetables 135

baked sea bass with olives and 88

chilli cornbread pie 67

cracked patatas bravas 27

Greek-style omelette 155

grilled salmon with avocado and sun-dried tomato dressing 89

hake with clams, fennel and cherry tomatoes 100

huevos rancheros 138

lamb rogan josh 75

Moroccan lamb tagine 64

onion tart with mozzarella and semi-sun dried tomatoes 154

oven-baked tomatoes with ratatouille 129

oven-roasted cannellini beans 173

oven-roasted Dublin Bay prawns

with chilli and 10

Puy lentil, red onion and sun-dried tomato salad 163

red onion, bean and tomato salad 15

roasted red pepper and tomato sauce 150

roasted stuffed aubergines with cherry tomatoes 127

tabbouleh salad 161

turkey moussaka 36–7

tortillas: quick quesadillas 144

tortilla chips 12

turkey enchiladas 56

trout: smoked fish platter 94

tuna: salad Niçoise 112

seared tuna with sweetcorn, red pepper and lime salsa 93

turkey: turkey enchiladas 56

turkey moussaka 36–7

vegetables: baked Mediterranean vegetables 135

chargrilled vegetable layered sandwich 120

garlic yoghurt cheese with crudités 140

stock 213

see also aubergines, peppers etc

Vietnamese beef noodle soup 81

Vietnamese spring rolls 25

Vietnamese-style grilled five-spice chicken thigh salad 51

vinaigrette, sherry 85

walnuts: Gorgonzola, pear and rocket salad 110

wine: red wine sauce 76–7

wonton wrappers: Swiss chard and ricotta ravioli 164

chicken and wild mushroom wontons 23–4

yoghurt: butterflied lamb with spiced mint and yoghurt rub 74

garlic yoghurt cheese 140